Seasonal Dishes from Murray's Century Farm

The
GROUNDS CAFÉ

—— RECIPES BY NICK VAN MELE ——

Library and Archives Canada Cataloguing in Publication

Title: The Grounds Café : seasonal dishes from Murray's Century Farm / recipes by Nick Van Mele.
Other titles: Seasonal dishes from Murray's Century Farm
Names: Van Mele, Nick, author.
Description: Includes index.
Identifiers: Canadiana 20230205070 | ISBN 9781989417607 (hardcover)
Subjects: LCSH: Grounds Café. | LCSH: Cooking—Newfoundland and Labrador—Portugal Cove-St. Philip's.
    | LCSH: Local foods—Newfoundland and Labrador—Portugal Cove-St. Philip's. | LCSH: Seasonal
    cooking—Newfoundland and Labrador—Portugal Cove-St. Philip's. | LCSH: Cooking, Canadian—
    Newfoundland and Labrador style. | LCGFT: Cookbooks.
Classification: LCC TX715.6 .V34 2023 | DDC 641.59718—dc23

MurraysGardens.com

Published by Boulder Books
Portugal Cove-St. Philip's, Newfoundland and Labrador
www.boulderbooks.ca

Design and layout: Todd Manning
Editor: Stephanie Porter
Copy editor: Iona Bulgin

Printed in China

We acknowledge the financial support of the Government of Newfoundland and
Labrador through the Department of Tourism, Culture, Industry and Innovation.

Seasonal Dishes from Murray's Century Farm

The
GROUNDS CAFÉ

—— RECIPES BY NICK VAN MELE ——

with contributions from Brian Kowalski, Cameron Murray,
Evan Murray, Michael Murray, Susan Murray, and Tim Murray

BOULDER
BOOKS

TABLE OF CONTENTS

SUMMER / 41

Summer salad with raspberries, currants, granola, basil pesto, and mint / 48

Sticky sesame cauliflower / 51

Beet fritter bowl / 54

Tomato salad with green olive vinaigrette and whipped feta / 59

Tomatoes on toast with arugula, aged cheddar, and Parmesan / 60

Tomato tart with basil pesto and mozzarella / 62

Charred zucchini, fennel, and tomato soup / 66

Black bean quinoa burger with coconut bacon and apple chutney / 69

Raspberry tart / 72

Fireweed jelly / 77

Rhubarb iced tea / 81

FALL / 83

Pickled fennel / 90

Eggplant and chanterelle pan pizza / 92

Wild mushrooms on a buttermilk biscuit with purple bean salad / 97

Baby beet salad with ricotta and grilled shishito peppers / 100

Warm fall harvest salad with roasted pumpkin, fall greens, and leek ash / 102

Gnocchi with peas, caramelized onions, and bacon / 105

Tomato jam / 109

Squash risotto with seared king oyster mushrooms / 110

Blueberry cheesecake bars / 114

Pin cherry crullers / 116

Dolgo apple fizz / 119

Apple butter / 120

WINTER / 123

MURRAY'S CENTURY FARM

A LONG RELATIONSHIP OF FOOD AND COMMUNITY

By Michael Murray

OUR ancestors arrived in Newfoundland in the early days of the 19th century, landing at Grates Cove as indentured servants. By 1820, our family had moved across the bay and established a subsistence farm at Murray's Pond, Portugal Cove. From these meagre beginnings, we created a thriving business centred around landscape design, horticulture, and organic vegetable production. That business has evolved into Murray's Garden Centre and The Grounds Cafe.

But let me take you back to one of my earliest memories—a moment that revealed to me the close connection between food and community.

I had been kept after school, forced to write, over and over, the answers to Catechism questions I had failed to memorize, until my arm ached. My punishment meant that I missed my school-bus ride, and I had to catch the 6 p.m. bus at Rawlins Cross back home to Portugal Cove. This was a new experience, and I was curious about who

Murray's, 1950s.

Murray's, 1970s.

would be travelling with me on such a cold miserable November evening.

This was the bus that transported working men and women of Portugal Cove home from their jobs in St. John's. I got on the bus and I walked down the aisle to the back to find a seat. Suddenly, I was challenged by a loud voice.

"Now! Who do we have here, b'ys? With his pressed blue blazer and his nice St. Bon's crest. Who are you, my son, and what are you doing out so late?"

"I'm Michael Murray, sir," I responded with trepidation.

"Oh," said the inquiring man. "You're named after your grandfather Mike Murray?"

"Yes, sir, I am."

"Come on, b'ys, move over and make some room for Mr. Murray."

The men shuffled around to make room for me in the back seat. "There you go. You all right?" the man asked as I squeezed in. "You know, my son, if it weren't for your crowd we would've all starved to death back in the old days."

There was a murmur of approval as I was offered a seat next to my inquirer, Fred Hussey. "Yes b'y! We'd help your grandfather and grandmother with the fall harvest for a share of the crop as payment." There was very little cash around those days and bartering vegetables and fish for labour was commonplace. "I remember your grandmother bringing huge pots of boiled dinner up to the field to feed everyone. The best meal of the day."

It made me feel proud to be associated with my family and recognized by the men on the bus that November evening as being part of my community's culture and well-being.

When I eventually got home, I explained my reasons for being so late. I told my father what Fred Hussey had said. "Fred only told you half the story," Father said, continuing with an obvious catch in his throat. "If it weren't for the Husseys, Mitchells, Earles, Allans, Churchills, Greeleys, Murphys, Drukens, and other families in the Cove who pitched in with us to plant, care for, and harvest those crops, we would've all starved to death."

My parents made sure that I understood the importance of community, co-operation, and the interdependence we all share in producing and presenting good food to ourselves and our neighbours.

Newfoundland and Labrador has come a long way from those harsh days of the dirty thrities, when the Great Depression crippled and broke families to the point of deprivation and starvation.

Today we are part of a global community. The customs and cultures of the world have come to our rugged shores. Some have come through an endless stream of information; others, displaced by war and retribution. But they have all enriched our lives and Newfoundland culture.

Our tastes have moved beyond salt fish, pickled pork, cabbage, and potatoes. Kimchi, ramen noodles, bean curd, and a wide range of international cuisine grace the tables of our homes and restaurants throughout the province.

It is our hope that this collection of tasty recipes, fused with the vegetables and fruits that come from the gardens and fields of Murray Meadows and the other farms of Newfoundland and Labrador, find a place in your home. I hope that this book will open your taste buds to an enriching culinary experience, one that we are proud to share with you at The Grounds Café.

Murray's, 2023.

MURRAY'S FARM HISTORICAL TIMELINE

ARRIVAL IN NEWFOUNDLAND
1820

Two Murray brothers, Patrick and Michael, depart Ireland and arrive in Grates Cove, Newfoundland, circa 1820.

A CENTURY FARM IN THE MAKING
1860

The Murrays begin to sell their farm produce. Fishing schooners from Conception Bay stop at Portugal Cove to purchase provisions, water, and freshened goats to take on their voyage. This type of agricultural production continues on the farm well into the next century.

MURRAY'S POND COUNTRY CLUB
1880

A portion of the Murray property is sold to a private group to form a fishing & country club.

ROADSIDE ATTRACTION
1978

Michael Murray (b. 1952) marries Susan Campbell (b. 1955) and opens one of the province's first roadside vegetable markets.

PROFESSIONAL DEVELOPMENT
2000

The company employs 30+ people, including horticulturists, designers, growers, arborists, landscapers, and general labourers. Michael becomes national president of Canadian Nursery and Landscape Association and promotes the landscape horticulture industry locally and abroad.

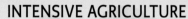

INTENSIVE AGRICULTURE
2012

Murray Meadows Farm is founded as an intensive vegetable farming operation. Produce is sold through Murray's Garden Centre, restaurants, and at the St. John's Farmers' Market.

1825 — NEW ROOTS
Patrick Murray, with his new bride, Mary Vey, move across Conception Bay to Portugal Cove to establish a homestead that would become Murray's Pond Farm.

1835 — BUILDING A LIFE
The land is cleared of trees and plowed. Suitable field stones are selected to construct the foundation of a root cellar and logs are used to construct the family house and barn. Many of these structures still exist today.

1980 — THE ART OF LANDSCAPING IN THE NORTHEAST AVALON
Murray's Landscape Services is founded and experiences rapid growth. Michael and Susan have three boys: Evan (b. 1982), Tim (b. 1985), and Cameron (b. 1988).

MURRAYS
Horticultural Services

1990 — NEW GROWTH
The roadside vegetable market evolves into Murray's Garden Centre where locally grown plants and other garden products are sold. Eventually the garden centre expands into a larger store and office space designed by Susan's father, architect Angus Campbell.

2017 — FROM FARM TO FORK
Murray's introduces The Grounds Café, a farm-to-fork restaurant with an upscale, innovative menu. Located in the café is a small art gallery featuring rug hookings, paintings, and other works from local artists.

A MESSAGE TO THE FUTURE
The only constant in business at Murray's is change. We continue to look for innovative ways to grow and diversify, while remaining rooted in our commitment to protecting and enhancing the land on which we live.

FARMERS, FORAGERS, FOODIES, FAMILY, AND FRIENDS

FARMERS

Farmers are the lifeblood of our operation. Following in the footsteps of the many Murrays who had farmed this land for generations, our farm took on a new life when Evan Murray and Brian Kowalski restarted food production in 2012, under the "Murray Meadows Farm" banner. Today, Nezar and Fatima Khalif and their Syrian-Canadian family help manage the day-to-day operations of the farm, ensuring a steady supply of fresh, delicious crops throughout the year.

FORAGERS

Our region is rich in wild foods that sustained entire communities long before modern agriculture was introduced here. Our restaurant is fortunate to have connections to these practices through people such as Shawn Dawson, a professional forager and wild-food harvester who regularly supplies our restaurant with a boreal bounty.

FOODIES

Our chefs work as hard as our farmers. The head chef of The Grounds Café, Nick van Mele, has a passion for cooking with ingredients grown or foraged fresh from our farm and forests. Through this passion, Nick and his team are constantly inspired to create delicious meals that give visitors a true taste of our farm.

FAMILY AND FRIENDS

From the neighbourhood regulars who frequent the cafe every day, to friends and family members always eager to provide encouragement, the Murray Farm and The Grounds Café would be nothing without the support of our broader community. We are fortunate to be surrounded by people who recognize the importance of local food production and show support through their participation and their patronage.

SPRING

S PRING is a dirty word in Newfoundland. Even as the sun's rays gain intensity and the days get longer, our maritime climate is terribly slow to warm. Furthermore, the confluence of oceanic and atmospheric currents that occur around the island can lead to intense spring storms, endless days of RDF (a.k.a. Rain, Drizzle, and Fog), and the occasional bout of June snow.

That being said, we do enjoy lovely days and, even on the most miserable ones, the eagerness to get the season started is more than enough to have us jump out of bed and get the day going. Even though it may feel like the middle of winter on certain days in March and April (and sometimes May!), seeds must be sown, cold frames (unheated greenhouses) must be covered, and fields must be turned. Before you know it, the growing season will have arrived.

Our farm uses minimal heating to produce vegetable and herb plants, as electricity and fuel are too pricey to make our farm financially viable if used in excess. While most seedlings are started in a heated structure, we use cold frames and frost blankets to protect our first crop plantings. By using passive heating systems like these, we can achieve our first harvest weeks, or even months, ahead of what would be possible by planting outside without protection.

The first harvests of mustard greens, scallions, hakurei turnips, and baby beets are eagerly anticipated by the café chefs. The opportunity to work with vibrant fresh vegetables is celebrated, as these first crops are often the sweetest and most tender of the year. The first bite is often enough to make you forget about the weather and make you appreciate the taste of spring.

COLD FRAMES

When it seems like spring is springing everywhere else but here in Newfoundland, it already feels like summer inside our cold frames. From March and through the chilly months of April, May, and June, on sunny spring days the temperature inside the cold frames can reach 30°C. At night, however, the inside temperature is not much different than that outside, often down to -5°C or colder. Yet we manage to grow a lot of vegetables inside the frames from the middle of April onward. Our farm greens and spring root vegetables are ready for harvest by mid-May.

The march to harvest starts in March (pun intended) when we cover the cold frames with plastic, helping to melt remaining snow and warming the ground within a few weeks. After direct seeding or transplanting seedlings, we cover the ground and plants with sheets of row cover. These lightweight fleece sheets trap the day's heat, keeping the area between it and the ground warm throughout the night. For the first few years using the cold frames, we tracked the temperature differences: one night it went to -5°C outside but, under the row cover, it was a balmy +5°C.

SPRING GREENS

After a winter of sad, mainland vegetables, fresh-picked bundles of lettuces, kale, chard, and arugula are a sight to behold. We start seeding transplants of lettuces, kale, chard, and bok choy at the beginning of March and transplant them in the cold frames in the last week of April. That week we also direct-seed arugula and mustard greens (a blend of very cold-hardy greens, including kale, arugula, mustard, tatsoi, and mizuna) for the first time, and continue to seed more each week. The greens are ready to harvest 4 to 6 weeks after transplanting, and it all tastes like fresh green magic.

ROOTS TOO!

Sweet spring greens aren't the only vegetables we grow early in the season. Many root vegetables love the cool temperatures as well. Radishes are easy to grow in the spring cold frame, as are the less-familiar new favourite, white spring turnips. Larger and milder than a radish, they are sweet and juicy and are great raw, roasted, or grilled Grounds-style. From seed, both are ready in a little more than a month. We also start our beets early. About five weeks after starting beet seed indoors, we transplant the tiny seedlings out in the cold frame. By mid-June, they're ready.

SPRING RECIPES

SPRING HARVEST SALAD

with honey vinaigrette, ricotta, poppy seeds, and rosemary oil

1 bag of locally grown
  salad greens
1 large carrot
1 bunch of radishes, sliced
1 shallot, sliced
1 tbsp poppy seeds

Rosemary oil
1 cup neutral oil
3 sprigs of rosemary

Honey vinaigrette
3 tbsp honey
1 lemon, juiced and zested
3 tbsp apple cider vinegar
½ shallot, minced
1 clove garlic, minced
1 tsp Dijon mustard
1 cup canola oil
Pinch of salt and pepper

Ricotta
4 cups whole milk
1 tbsp white vinegar
1 lemon, juiced
1 tsp salt
1 tsp honey

This is a beautiful presentation of the best of spring, combined with pantry items from past seasons.

First make the ricotta. You can buy it from the store, but it is easy to do at home. In a medium pot, bring the milk up to a scald—just before boiling, or 85°C if you have a thermometer handy. Take off the heat and add the vinegar, lemon juice, and salt. Stir gently until the clear whey fully separates and loose curds start to form. Strain off the whey through a cheesecloth or fine mesh sieve. Let chill for at least 2 hours or overnight. Add 1 teaspoon honey to the cooled ricotta and more salt to taste.

The rosemary oil is a simple pantry item that we make with the last harvest of rosemary from the fall and winter. Gently warm any neutral oil with a few sprigs of rosemary to infuse. If you do not have access to rosemary, a good-quality extra virgin olive oil is a fine substitute.

Whisk all ingredients for the honey vinaigrette in a bowl and check the seasoning. Add more vinegar, honey, and salt to your taste.

To assemble the salad, use a vegetable peeler to slice long ribbons of carrot. Mix the carrot ribbons with the greens, radishes, and shallot. Toss with a few teaspoons of honey vinaigrette and half of the poppy seeds.

Place in a bowl and finish by crumbling the ricotta on top with a drizzle of rosemary oil and the rest of the poppy seeds.

KALE SALAD

with apple-walnut vinaigrette, kohlrabi, and seedy granola

1 bag of baby kale mix, washed
**1 small kohlrabi, peeled and cut
into matchsticks**

Apple-walnut vinaigrette
⅓ cup toasted walnuts
**⅓ cup unsweetened applesauce
or apple butter (page 120)**
⅓ cup apple juice or water
⅓ cup apple cider vinegar
2 tbsp canola oil
2 tbsp maple syrup
Pinch of cayenne
Salt and pepper

Seedy granola
1 cup gluten-free rolled oats
½ cup pumpkin seeds
½ cup sunflower seeds
¼ cup sesame seeds
¼ cup chia seeds
¼ cup maple syrup
½ tsp salt
Pinch of cinnamon
Pinch of cayenne

*This vegan and gluten-free salad works well as a full meal
or a fresh side dish. The kohlrabi complements the granola,
as both add sweet crunch to the dish.*

Place all ingredients for the apple-walnut vinaigrette in a
blender and purée until smooth and silky. Check seasoning and adjust to taste.

Toss the seedy granola ingredients in a mixing bowl and
spread on a parchment-lined baking sheet. Bake at 325°F
for 30 minutes, stirring every 10 minutes until golden.

Toss the baby kale with a generous amount of the vinaigrette and a handful of julienned kohlrabi. Finish with a
couple of tablespoons of granola.

TOFU LETTUCE WRAPS

with spicy peanut sauce, sticky rice, radish, pea shoots, and cashews

1 package (350 g / 16 oz) firm organic tofu
Pickle brine or hot pepper brine
¼ cup potato starch or cornstarch

1 to 2 heads of Boston bibb or romaine lettuce
1 bunch of radishes

1 handful of pea shoots
1 handful of fresh mint leaves
¼ cup toasted crushed cashews

Sticky rice
1 cup glutinous rice
2 cups water
¼ cup rice vinegar
¼ cup white sugar

Spicy peanut sauce
¾ cup peanut butter
3 tbsp tamari or soy sauce
⅓ cup rice vinegar
1 tbsp brown sugar
3 tbsp sambal garlic chili paste (or your favourite hot sauce)
1 tsp sesame oil
1 lime
1 thumb of grated ginger
1 garlic clove, minced
⅓ cup water

When spring hits, we start to crave light, crisp, and fresh meals, which perfectly sums up this make-your-own-style dish.

Cut the tofu into bite-sized cubes, place in a bowl, and add a good splash of pickle brine or hot pepper brine. Let marinate while you prepare the other ingredients.

Rinse the glutinous rice under cold running water until the water runs clear. Use a medium pot with a tight-fitting lid. Add the rice and 2 cups cold water. Bring to a boil. Boil, uncovered, for 2 minutes. Turn heat to low, and simmer for 5 minutes. Place the cover on the rice and let simmer another 2 minutes. Turn off the heat; leave the pot on the burner. Do not remove the lid. Let steam for 10 minutes. While the rice is steaming, place the rice vinegar and sugar in a small pot and reduce by half. This seasoning will turn the rice into sweet, tart, sticky rice. Add the reduction to fully cooked rice and stir together with a fork.

Continued on next page

From previous page

Place all ingredients for the peanut sauce in a mixing bowl and whisk together until smooth. Set aside.

Select and remove full leaves of lettuce and soak them in cold water for several minutes to firm them up while you prep the rest of the ingredients.

Wash and dry the radishes and cut into thin slices. You can add the radish greens to the tofu at the end of the cooking process if you would like.

Drain the marinade from the tofu and toss the tofu with the potato starch. Heat 1 to 2 tablespoons neutral oil in a medium frying pan and cook the tofu in batches, adding more oil as necessary, until crispy. Place the cooked tofu on a paper-towel-lined plate, then toss it in some of the spicy peanut sauce when ready to serve.

This dish is best served family style: let everyone build their own. It also packs up well for a quick lunch to-go.

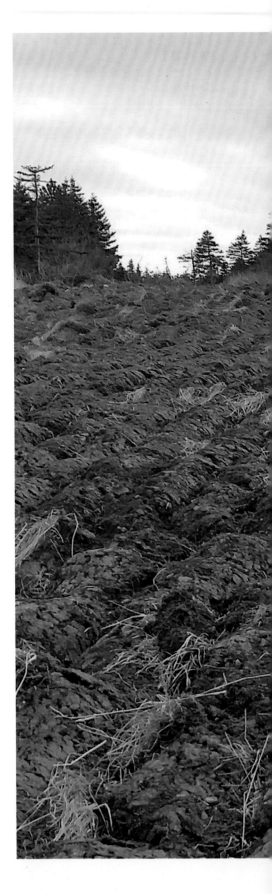

CHIVE AND CHEESE CURD SCONES

⅔ cup cold unsalted butter
1 egg
½ cup buttermilk
1¾ cups all-purpose flour
1 tbsp salt
½ tbsp white sugar
2¼ tsp baking powder
½ tsp baking soda
1½ cups cheese curds
2 bunches of fresh
  chives, chopped
Flaked sea salt and pepper

1 egg + 1 tbsp water or milk
  for egg wash

An heirloom patch of chives comes back every spring in an old vegetable patch next to the café. They grow in abundance for a few weeks before they turn to flower and seed— then they're gone. Being able to snip chives by the bunch as we need them is one of our favourite parts of spring. Pairing fresh chives with cheese curds makes this pastry irresistible.

Mix the flour, salt, sugar, baking powder, and baking soda in a medium mixing bowl. Set aside. Use a cheese grater to grate the cold butter, and rub it into the dry mix. Mix the buttermilk and egg in a separate bowl, then add to the flour mixture. Add the cheese curds and chives. Roughly mix to make a loose dough. Do not overmix or knead. You want to keep small chunks of butter to create air pockets while the scones bake.

Preheat the oven to 375°F and roll out the scone dough on a well-floured surface to about ½ inch thick. Cut into squares. Place on a heavy baking sheet lined with parchment paper. Whisk together the egg and water or milk and lightly brush the scones with this egg wash. Sprinkle a little flaked sea salt and cracked pepper on each scone.

Bake for 12 to 18 minutes or until golden.

OYSTER MUSHROOM AND CHIVE TARTLET WITH GARLIC CREAM

Pie dough
2½ cups flour
1 cup butter, grated
1 tsp salt
¼ cup cold water

1 lb oyster mushrooms
2 tbsp unsalted butter
1 lemon
2 bunches of fresh chives, chopped
1 egg

Garlic cream
4 cups whipping cream
1 head of garlic
2 tbsp unsalted butter
1 shallot, sliced
1 tsp Dijon mustard
½ tsp chili flakes
Salt and pepper
Olive oil

This delicious savoury pastry highlights local oyster mushrooms and spring chives.

Make the pie dough. Add flour, salt, and grated butter to a mixing bowl. Using your hands, rub the ingredients together to form small, pea-shaped pieces of butter. Add cold water and form into a ball, being careful not to over mix. Press the dough into a disc shape, wrap in plastic wrap, and refrigerate for 1 hour before using.

Roast the head of garlic: Cut off the top so that each clove is just exposed, place on a square of aluminum foil, drizzle with oil, and fold the foil to cover the entire head. Roast at 350°F for 30 to 40 minutes until golden. Let cool for a few minutes. When cool enough to handle, pinch the base of the head of garlic to push out the roasted garlic; it should be a paste-like consistency.

In a medium pot, melt the butter and sauté the sliced shallot with the chili flakes, salt, and pepper. Add the cream, roasted garlic, and Dijon mustard. Reduce heat to a simmer and reduce by half.

Trim the oyster mushrooms and clean off any dirt; depending on the size, you may be able to pull them apart by hand into pieces. Heat a skillet and sauté the mushrooms with butter. You don't need to fully cook the mushrooms, because they will be baked. The goal here is to start the cooking process and extract some moisture.

Continued on page 20

From page 18

Roll out the quiche dough to a large square, ⅛ inch thick. Cut into six to eight 4-inch squares. Make an egg wash by whisking 1 egg with a splash of water. Lightly brush the edges of the pastry square with the egg wash.

Place a heaping teaspoon of the roasted garlic cream in the centre of each square and pinch over the edges to create a crust. Add a pinch of chives and a heaping tablespoon of the sautéed mushrooms.

Brush the crust with a little more egg wash and sprinkle salt and pepper on top. Chill the tarts for 20 minutes.

Bake the tarts for 18 to 22 minutes at 400°F or until golden.

Finish the tarts with a heaping teaspoon of fresh chopped chives and a drizzle of lemon juice and olive oil.

BEET TACOS

with salsa verde, pine nuts, bean spread, arugula, and hot sauce

Corn tortillas
3 large beets
1 cup baby arugula
Hot sauce of choice
¼ cup toasted pine nuts
Extra herbs for garnishing

Bean spread
½ cup dried red kidney beans
   or 1 can (19 oz / 540 ml)
   prepared kidney beans,
   rinsed and drained
¼ cup unsalted butter
¼ cup cream cheese
1 shallot
1 garlic clove
1 tsp ground cumin
Salt and pepper

Salsa verde
1 tbsp chopped capers
1 tbsp chopped pickled peppers
1 shallot, diced finely
2 cloves garlic, diced finely
½ bunch of parsley,
   chopped finely
½ bunch of cilantro,
   chopped finely
1 tbsp chopped mint
½ cup extra virgin olive oil
2 limes, juiced and zested

A farm fresh twist on taco night.

Soak the kidney beans in water overnight if you are using dried beans. Drain. Place in a medium pot, cover with fresh water, and boil until tender. In a frying pan, sauté the onions and garlic in butter until soft and translucent. Season with salt and pepper and add the cumin. Add the beans to the mixture and then transfer to a food processor. Blend until smooth. If you do not have a food processor, mash the mixture into a spread using a fork. Check seasoning and set aside.

For the salsa verde, place the diced shallot and garlic in a medium bowl and add ½ teaspoon salt and some pepper. Let sit for a few minutes and then stir in the rest of the ingredients. Check for seasoning at the end.

Prepare the beets using the beet frites method (page 130).

Warm the tortillas a little before serving, spread some of the bean mixture in the middle, and top with crispy beets, a tablespoon of salsa verde, a few sprigs of baby arugula, pine nuts, and any extra herb trimmings you have around. Serve with hot sauce.

SNOW CRAB SALAD

with brown butter vinaigrette, torn croutons, pickled radish, and chives

1 snow crab (1½ to 2½ lbs)
4 cups romaine hearts,
   cleaned and torn
1 bunch of radishes
1 cup white vinegar
¼ cup white sugar
1 bunch of fresh chives
Sea salt
Half a loaf of sourdough bread
   (or other day-old bread)
Olive oil

Brown butter vinaigrette
½ cup brown butter
   (page 155)
½ cup canola oil
¼ cup red wine vinegar
¼ cup honey
1 lemon, juiced and zested
1 shallot, minced
1 garlic clove, minced
Salt and pepper

Snow crab season is short but sweet. Snow crab is a special ingredient that we're always happy to receive at the café.

Clean and cut the radishes into small wedges. Bring 1 cup white vinegar and ¼ cup white sugar to a boil and pour over the radishes. Let cool.

In a pot of boiling salted water, cook the crab for 8 to 10 minutes. Let cool. Cut apart with a pair of heavy-duty kitchen shears and remove the crab meat; set aside.

Whisk all vinaigrette ingredients together in a mixing bowl. Check the seasoning and keep in a warm place until ready to use. If the vinaigrette cools, bring it back to room temperature or warm slightly in a small pot.

Preheat oven to 375°F. Carefully tear the sourdough into small pieces. Toss it in a bowl with a generous amount of olive oil, salt, and pepper. Spread bread pieces on a baking sheet and toast for 10 to 12 minutes, stirring halfway through until golden on the outside but still soft in the middle.

To assemble the salad, toss the romaine hearts, croutons, and pickled radishes with 2 or 3 tablespoons of vinaigrette in a large bowl. Top with pieces of snow crab. Drizzle a little more of the brown butter vinaigrette over the crab. Sprinkle with chopped chives and flaked Newfoundland sea salt.

BUCKWHEAT NOODLE BOWL

4 portions of buckwheat noodles
½ cup green onions, chopped
½ lb fresh shiitake mushrooms
2 tbsp toasted sesame seeds
2 limes
¼ cup peanuts, toasted and crushed
Cilantro and shiso for garnish

Pickled carrots
2 to 3 large carrots, peeled and
   cut into matchsticks
1 cup white vinegar
¼ cup white sugar

Miso-ginger sauce
¼ cup peeled, chopped ginger
½ cup miso paste
2 tbsp toasted sesame seeds
3 tbsp tamari
6 tbsp maple syrup
⅔ cup rice vinegar
1 tbsp sesame oil
1 tsp sriracha
Salt and pepper

Served chilled with miso-ginger sauce, pickled carrots, sesame seeds, lime, and peanuts, this is a satisfying and refreshing spring dish.

In a large pot of boiling water, cook the buckwheat noodles for 3 to 5 minutes until soft and chewy. Strain and place the noodles in an ice bath.

Place all ingredients for the miso-ginger sauce in a blender and purée until smooth. Check seasoning. Set aside.

To pickle the carrots, boil the vinegar and sugar and pour over the carrots. Let cool; refrigerate.

Slice the shiitake mushrooms into thin strips and sauté them on medium heat with a little oil. Add 1 to 2 tablespoons water if they start to get dry.

Toss the buckwheat noodles in a few tablespoons of the miso-ginger sauce; add more sauce to taste. Place the dressed noodles in a serving dish and layer the pickled carrots, sautéed shiitakes, and spring onions on top. Finish with toasted sesame seeds, crushed peanuts, a lime wedge, and fresh herbs.

HANDMADE PASTA
WITH NETTLE PESTO AND CURED RADISH

Pasta dough
2 cups pasta flour or all-purpose flour, plus extra for dusting
3 eggs
Salt
1 tsp olive oil

Nettle pesto
⅔ cup blanched nettle tops (about 8 cups fresh stinging nettle tops)
2 tbsp toasted almonds
2 tbsp Parmesan cheese
3 garlic cloves
2 tsp chili flakes
⅓ cup extra virgin olive oil

Cured radish
1 cup radishes, quartered
1 tbsp salt
1 tbsp white sugar
2 juniper berries, ground
1 spruce tip
2 alder catkins, ground

Prepare the radishes the day before you want to make this dish. Combine the salt, sugar, juniper berries, spruce tip, and alder catkins to make a dry cure. Toss with the cut radishes and allow to cure, covered, in the refrigerator overnight. The next day, rinse off the cure and let the radishes dry on a cloth or paper towel until ready to be used.

To make the pasta dough, place the flour in a mound on a large clean work surface. Create a well in the middle and crack the eggs into the depression. Add a pinch of salt and the olive oil. Stir around the edge of the wet ingredients with a fork to gradually work in the flour. When the ingredients are fully incorporated, knead the dough for 10 minutes. It should be a stiff dough but not impossible to knead. If the dough is too dry or too wet, adjust with a few drops of water or a bit of flour. Roll into a ball and cover with plastic wrap. Refrigerate for 30 minutes.

Carefully blanch the nettles in lightly salted boiling water for 30 seconds, using tongs or gloves to handle the nettles. Blanching the nettles eliminates their ability to sting. Transfer the nettles to an ice bath, then drain. Roughly chop them and set aside.

Coarsely chop the garlic and almonds in a food processor. Add the grated Parmesan, nettles, and a pinch of salt. Drizzle in the olive oil 1 tablespoon at a time until the pesto reaches the desired consistency.

Continued on next page

From previous page

For this recipe, I use a long thin noodle shape—usually linguine—but you can make any shape you would like. Roll the pasta out using a pasta sheet roller to setting 5, keeping the dough well floured the whole time. Roll the dough sheet into a manageable log and cut into thin noodles, pulling apart and flouring the noodles as necessary to ensure that they do not stick together.

Bring a large pot of lightly salted water to a boil. In a large frying pan set to medium-low heat, sauté the cured radishes in a mixture of oil and butter until they start to turn golden and they are cooked through. Cook the noodles in boiling water for 2 to 4 minutes until al dente, depending on the thickness. Strain the noodles and reserve ¼ cup of the pasta water. Add the noodles, pasta water, and a few tablespoons pesto to the frying pan with the cooked cured radishes. If you have radish greens, toss them in at this point.

Simmer until thickened. Finish with a knob of butter, a squeeze of fresh lemon, and grated Parmesan.

LOBSTER EGGS BENNY
ON A BUTTERMILK BISCUIT

1 fresh lobster (about 1½ lbs)
Arugula and chives for garnish

Buttermilk biscuits
4 cups all-purpose flour
½ lb cold unsalted butter
½ tsp baking soda
2 tsp salt
2 tbsp baking powder
2⅓ cups buttermilk
1 egg + 1 tbsp water or milk
for egg wash

Hollandaise sauce
2 egg yolks
½ cup warm clarified butter
1 tsp white wine vinegar
reduction (optional)
1 tsp lemon juice
Pinch of cayenne
Salt to taste

For the clarified butter, slowly melt 1 pound butter in a small saucepan without boiling. Set aside and let settle for a few minutes. The clarified butter will rise to the top and the milk solids will settle in the bottom. Carefully pour the clarified butter into a separate container and keep warm.

Make a white wine vinegar reduction by simmering ¼ cup white wine vinegar with 1 bay leaf and ½ teaspoon peppercorns. Reduce by half and set aside.

Cook the lobster in a large pot of salted water for 10 minutes, let cool, and take the lobster meat out of the shell. Set aside in a bowl.

Mix the flour, baking soda, baking powder, and salt in a large bowl. Grate the butter with a cheese grater, then rub it into the flour mixture by hand, breaking up the butter into pea-sized pieces. Add the buttermilk, mixing by hand and scooping the flour from the bottom to the top. Repeat until all the buttermilk is incorporated, without overmixing.

Cover with plastic wrap and let rest 15 minutes. Roll out the dough to roughly 1 inch thick on a well-floured surface. Use a cookie cutter to cut out round biscuits or a knife to cut into squares.

Continued on next page

From previous page

Place the biscuits on a parchment-lined baking sheet, leaving 1 inch or so of space around each one. In a small bowl, whisk together 1 egg with 1 tablespoon water or milk and brush the top of the biscuits with this egg wash. Bake at 375°F for 18 to 24 minutes or until golden. These biscuits can be made ahead and re-warmed when ready to assemble.

Set up a double boiler to make the hollandaise sauce. Warm the clarified butter in a small saucepan. Place the egg yolks and white wine reduction in a bowl that fits over the top of a double boiler. Place over the double boiler and whisk the ingredients until the liquid becomes slightly pale and frothy and increases in volume.

Use a small ladle to stream the clarified butter into the egg mixture while whisking vigorously. Continue whisking until all the butter has been incorporated. Add lemon juice to "break" the sauce and a few drops of water if necessary to loosen it. Add a pinch of cayenne and season generously with salt. Cover the sauce and place in a warm spot until ready to serve.

To assemble: cut each biscuit in half and toast in the oven. Heat the lobster meat in a small saucepan with a little butter. Place a handful of arugula sprigs dressed in olive oil, salt, and pepper on each side of the biscuit. Scoop mounds of lobster meat on each, drizzling some of the extra butter on top. Drape a small ladleful of hollandaise over the top and finish with fresh chopped chives and flaked sea salt.

GLUTEN-FREE RHUBARB BARS

Base
1½ cups gluten-free flour
1½ cups almond flour
⅔ cup white sugar
½ lb unsalted butter, diced

Topping
¼ cup brown sugar
1 cup sliced almonds
3 cups fresh, diced rhubarb
¼ cup white sugar

Rhubarb, a versatile, abundant crop throughout the spring and summer, lends itself perfectly to this gluten-free treat.

In a medium bowl, mix the base ingredients with your hands to a consistent cookie-dough-like texture.

Press half of the base mixture into an 8 by 6-inch baking dish lined with parchment paper. Bake at 350°F for 10 minutes or until slightly golden on top.

While the base is baking, toss the diced rhubarb with ¼ cup sugar. Spread the rhubarb on the baked base and bake for another 6 to 8 minutes or until the rhubarb begins to soften and release moisture.

Add ¼ cup brown sugar and 1 cup sliced almonds to the remaining base mixture. Crumble over the rhubarb layer and bake until golden, about 10 minutes.

SUMMER

S UMMER is a cherished—but extremely busy—time on the farm and in the café. At the start of summer, we are firing on all cylinders! All our winter planning and push through the spring is starting to pay off. Regular harvests of hardy crops are possible, unprotected outdoor plantings and seedings can take place, and warm weather crops can be cycled into the cold frames. The café is usually humming with activity as we kick into the busiest part of the year, with locals and tourists flocking to the café and gardens to enjoy a taste of Newfoundland summer. As well as providing prepared meals through the café, we also begin farm-gate sales in the summer, allowing customers to purchase our farm produce directly. Often our vegetables can be purchased within only an hour or two of harvesting.

Without a doubt, one of the most satisfying moments of the summer is the arrival of the first ripe tomato. We dedicate a lot of time and labour to our tomatoes, but the value of the crop and the first bite of a sweet, juicy tomato make it all worth it.

As the summer progresses, our greenhouses let us feel like we are a little closer to the equator! Heat-lovers such as squash, peppers, cucumbers, and basil take off, leaving the chefs at the café wondering what they're going to do with 100 pounds of zucchini and bushels upon bushels of jalapenos!

We all know that warm weather is fleeting on the east coast of Newfoundland. No matter how busy the summer is, it's important to take some time for yourself and enjoy life away from the farm. Grabbing a picnic lunch to-go from the café and hitting the pond with an inner tube and a local microbrew beer provides the perfect respite after a long day.

URRAY MEADOWS FARM

FLATBREAD W. SQUASH PURÉE, CURLIED VEG.
YOGURT, TOASTED ALMONDS
$ 11 * *VEGETARIAN OPTION*

TOMATOES

Tomatoes are our number-one crop. They seem to be everyone's favourite and we never have enough. Started from seed in February, we plant our tomato seedlings in a heated greenhouse in April. Fertilized carefully with specific nutrients and meticulously pruned, by June we are picking ripe flavourful tomatoes for the café. A few weeks later, hundreds of pounds are picked every week.

Tomatoes are our most labour-intensive crop. We grow vining, or indeterminate, tomatoes. We prune each plant to one or two vines; all other suckers are plucked off every week, as are all the leaves below the fruit clusters. As the vines grow, they are held up with twine attached to a cable. As the vines grow longer, we lower the twine and slide them down the cable, so as the vines grow, their bases lie

horizontal before growing up. At the end of the season, some vines are over 15 feet long. Clusters of tomatoes are picked every 8 to 10 inches of vine. They need to be fed frequently and watered every day. They also need to be monitored for diseases to be pruned off before they spread to the other plants—a danger especially in damp weather.

PEPPERS

Another crop we never seem to have enough space for is peppers. There are so many colours, shapes, and heat levels, and everyone has a favourite. Peppers do surprisingly well in our cool climate planted inside cold frames. We try to get them out as close to July 1 as possible, when the nights are generally warmer. We plant through black fabric that helps warm the ground and trap moisture. As peppers are not heavy feeders, a few handfuls of organic fertilizer every month is all they need to pump peppers out all summer and fall long. Given protection with row cover from early morning fall frosts, they will continue to produce fruit until they freeze. Bell peppers such as King of the North, as well as any jalapeno or cayenne, do really well. We've successfully grown shishitos, padrons, habaneros, and more. Recently we have started growing Carmen, a long red sweet pepper. Wow, what a flavour in those!

SUMMER RECIPES

SUMMER SALAD

with raspberries, currants, granola, basil pesto, and mint

Salad
Freshly harvested salad greens, washed
2 to 3 radishes, sliced
½ cucumber, sliced
Raspberries
Red and white currants
Basil leaves
River mint
Shaved Parmesan

Vinaigrette
2 lemons, juiced and zested
1 tsp Dijon mustard
1 tbsp apple cider vinegar
1 tbsp honey
1 cup canola oil
1 tbsp extra virgin olive oil
1 clove garlic, minced
½ shallot, minced
Pinch of salt and pepper

Granola
½ cup rolled oats
¼ cup black sesame seeds
¼ cup pumpkin seeds
¼ cup sliced almonds
¼ cup sunflower seeds
¼ cup maple syrup
1 tbsp brown sugar
1½ tsp salt

The goal of this salad is to show off the summer's bounty. Use the ingredients that you have, substitute other berries if necessary, add cherry tomatoes if available—you get the idea!

First, make the granola. Preheat the oven to 325°F. Mix all granola ingredients in a large bowl. Spread out evenly on a parchment-lined baking sheet and toast for about 30 minutes, while checking and stirring every 10 minutes. When golden, remove from the oven and let cool, then break up any large clusters.

To make the vinaigrette, place the minced shallot, garlic, salt, and pepper in a mixing bowl. Let it sit for a few minutes and then add the Dijon mustard, vinegar, lemon juice, honey, and olive oil and whisk. Slowly drizzle in the canola oil while whisking vigorously to emulsify the vinaigrette.

To assemble the salad, toss the salad greens, radishes, and cucumber with a few tablespoons of lemon vinaigrette and a pinch of salt and pepper. Place in a serving dish and cover with a handful of granola. Top with currants, raspberries, shaved Parmesan, basil leaves, mint leaves, edible flowers if you have them, and a drizzle of extra virgin olive oil.

STICKY SESAME CAULIFLOWER

1 head of cauliflower,
   cut in bite-sized florets
2 tbsp olive oil
1 red onion, sliced thinly
3 baby carrots, sliced,
   or 1 large carrot, julienned
1 cayenne or Thai chili, sliced
1 head of lettuce,
   cut and washed
4 cups steamed rice
2 radishes, sliced
¼ cup chopped cilantro and mint
Toasted sesame seeds

Pickling liquid
1 cup white vinegar
⅓ cup white sugar
⅓ cup water
⅓ tsp salt

Lime aioli
1 cup aioli (page 130)
   or purchased mayonnaise
2 limes, juiced and zested
Pinch of salt

This sweet and spicy summer dish packs a lot of flavour. You can serve it as a main dish with lettuce and rice, or serve the sticky sesame cauliflower on its own as an appetizer.

Pickle the red onions and carrots. Place the sliced red onions in a heatproof container and the sliced carrots in another. In a small saucepan, combine the white vinegar, sugar, water, and salt. Whisk to dissolve the sugar, and bring to a boil. Pour the boiling pickling liquid evenly over the carrots and the onions. Cover and set aside to cool.

To make the lime aioli, combine 1 cup homemade aioli or mayonnaise with the lime juice, zest, and salt. Whisk together and set aside.

Place all ingredients for the sticky sesame sauce (not including the cornstarch mixture) in a medium saucepan. Bring to a boil and then reduce to a simmer for 15 minutes. Whisk in the cornstarch mixture to thicken, and set aside.

Preheat the oven to 400°F. Toss the cauliflower florets with 2 tablespoons olive oil, salt, and pepper. Place on a baking sheet and roast for 15 to 20 minutes, until slightly crispy and golden.

Continued on next page

Continued on next page

From previous page

Sticky sesame sauce

**1 thumb of fresh ginger,
    peeled and chopped**

2 cloves garlic, chopped

½ cup tamari or soy sauce

½ cup rice vinegar

**1 cup vegetable broth,
    chicken stock, or water**

2 tbsp sesame oil

1 cup brown sugar

½ cup ketchup

**2 tbsp cornstarch mixed
    with ¼ cup water**

From previous page

To assemble, place a spoonful of steamed rice per bowl and add a handful of the washed lettuce and a few slices of radish. Toss the roasted cauliflower with the sticky sesame sauce and spoon a portion on the rice and lettuce. Use a spoon to drizzle lime aioli over each and then add a few pieces of pickled red onions and pickled carrots. Sprinkle a pinch of red chilis and sesame seeds on each. Finish with chopped cilantro and mint.

BEET FRITTER BOWL

2 cups grated beet
½ cup grated carrot
1 cup grated firm tofu
⅓ cup corn flour
¼ cup cornstarch
2 tsp ground cumin
½ tsp ground cardamom
1 tsp sumac
1 tsp salt
2 tbsp sesame seeds
⅓ cup water
Oil for frying
Extra corn flour for coating
  the beet fritters before frying

Turmeric hummus
1 cup dry chickpeas or
  1 19 oz (540 ml) can chickpeas,
  drained and rinsed
2 tbsp tahini
1 clove garlic
¼ cup extra virgin olive oil
2 tbsp honey
1 lemon, juice and zest
2 tsp turmeric
1 tsp paprika
1 tsp ground cumin
Salt and pepper

Apple-walnut vinaigrette
  (page 10)

Quinoa or green salad to serve

Beets are one of the most abundant and versatile vegetables that we grow at the Murray farm and we're always dreaming up new ways to serve them at the café.

Boil the dry chickpeas in a large pot of water until tender. Reserve some of the chickpea liquid to add to the hummus. If using canned chickpeas, skip this step.

While the chickpeas are cooking, combine the grated beets, carrots, and tofu in a large bowl. Add the spices and water and mix well. Refrigerate the mixture for 20 to 30 minutes.

To make the turmeric hummus, place the cooked chickpeas along with the rest of the ingredients and 2 to 3 tablespoons of the reserved chickpea liquid in a blender or food processor. Blend until smooth, adding more of the reserved chickpea liquid as needed. Set the turmeric hummus aside.

Preheat the oven to 350°F. Cover the bottom of a large frying pan with canola oil and heat to medium high on a stovetop burner.

Use a spoon to portion out bite-sized fritters and then toss them in a bowl with the corn flour to coat. Carefully place the fritters in the hot oil without crowding the pan. I usually do 6 to 8 fritters at a time depending on the size of the pan.

Continued on page 56

From page 54

Cook for a few minutes on each side, rotating as needed. When the beet fritters are golden brown, place them on a parchment-lined baking sheet and bake for an additional 15 minutes in the preheated oven.

Serve the beet fritters on their own with the turmeric hummus or prepare a simple quinoa salad with fresh squeezed lemon, olive oil, chopped herbs, and any other available vegetables. We like to use fresh sliced radish.

To plate, dollop a spoonful of the turmeric hummus on the bottom of a plate and spread it around to create a nest for the fritters. Place the beet fritters on top and drizzle with the apple-walnut dressing. Spoon a simple quinoa salad or other fresh vegetable salad beside the hummus, and enjoy.

TOMATO SALAD WITH GREEN OLIVE VINAIGRETTE AND WHIPPED FETA

6 tomatoes,
   cut into wedges
2 hakurei turnips,
   cut into small wedges
3 or 4 shishito peppers, sliced
2 cups tatsoi, washed
Fresh mint, chopped

Green olive vinaigrette
¼ cup green olives
   (we used Castelvetrano)
1 shallot
1 clove garlic
¼ cup apple cider vinegar
½ cup canola oil
2 tbsp olive oil
1 tbsp honey
1 lemon, zested and juiced
Salt and pepper

Whipped feta
1 cup feta cheese
½ cup heavy whipping cream

This is a fun twist on the classic Greek salad. The green olive vinaigrette balances out the beautiful fresh produce and pairs well with the creamy whipped feta.

To make the green olive vinaigrette, remove the pits from the green olives and chop roughly. Finely mince the shallots and garlic. Place the chopped olives, shallots, and garlic in a mixing bowl and season with salt and pepper. Add the vinegar, oils, honey, lemon juice, and zest and whisk together. Add additional salt and pepper if needed.

Place the feta cheese and whipping cream in a blender and mix until smooth.

Place the tomatoes, turnips, peppers, and tatsoi in a mixing bowl and ladle in the vinaigrette to taste. Use a spoon to spread a heavy dollop of whipped feta around the inside and rim of a serving bowl. Place the veggies in the middle, add a little more vinaigrette, and top with fresh chopped mint.

TOMATOES ON TOAST

with arugula, aged cheddar, and Parmesan

1 baguette or other fresh bread

2 large beefsteak or
heirloom tomatoes, sliced

2 cups arugula

¼ cup fresh basil leaves

½ cup grated aged cheddar

2 to 3 tbsp shaved Parmesan

2 tbsp extra virgin olive oil

Flaked sea salt and pepper

1 lemon, juiced

A beautifully simple lunch idea.

Cut the baguette in 3- to 4-inch-long pieces and then slice each piece in half.

Set the oven to broil. Cover each half of the bread with aged cheddar, place on an aluminum-foil-lined baking sheet, and broil until the cheese melts.

Slice the tomatoes. Toss the arugula and basil with lemon juice and olive oil, and season with salt and pepper.

Layer the sliced tomatoes on top of the bread, season with flaked salt and ground pepper. Cover the tomatoes with the dressed greens, then sprinkle shaved Parmesan over each half. Drizzle with more olive oil.

TOMATO TART WITH BASIL PESTO AND MOZZARELLA

1 recipe pie dough (page 18)
3 to 4 large tomatoes, sliced
1 8 oz fresh mozzarella ball,
    sliced

Basil pesto
2 cups fresh basil
¼ cup grated Parmesan
¼ cup canola oil
¼ cup extra virgin olive oil
2 cloves garlic, minced
½ lemon, juiced
¼ cup pine nuts or
    toasted almonds (optional)
Pinch of chili flakes
Salt and pepper to taste

This delectable pastry can be served as an appetizer or with a salad for a beautiful lunch. You'll need an 8- to 10-inch tart mould or pie plate to form the tomato tart.

On a floured work surface, roll out the pie dough to a flat circle about ⅛ inch thick, making sure that it is wide enough to cover the tart mould or pie plate. Use butter or cooking spray to grease the tart mould, then place the pie dough over it, pressing it down into the creases. Trim any excess pie dough, then chill for 30 minutes.

Place all the basil pesto ingredients in a blender or food processor and blend until smooth. Check for seasoning, and add salt and pepper to taste. Set aside.

Preheat the oven to 350°F. Cut a piece of parchment paper to line the inside of the tart shell and use weights or dried beans to weigh it down. Bake the shell for 10 to 12 minutes until it starts to turn golden and a little flaky, then remove the parchment and pie weights and bake for another 3 minutes.

To assemble the tart, spread about 3 tablespoons basil pesto in the bottom of the tart, then layer the tomato and mozzarella slices in a spiral pattern, alternating between 2 slices of tomato and 1 slice of mozzarella. Fill the entire tart and drizzle with a little extra olive oil. Bake for 12 to 15 minutes. Serve warm, garnished with fresh basil leaves.

CHARRED ZUCCHINI, FENNEL, AND TOMATO SOUP

2 large zucchini, sliced

2 to 3 bulbs of fennel, sliced

4 tomatoes, chopped

1 medium onion, diced

4 cloves garlic, minced

¼ cup extra virgin olive oil

4 cups vegetable broth

1 tsp red wine vinegar

½ tsp chili flakes

Salt and pepper

Charring the zucchini and fennel adds depth to this simple summer soup.

First, char the sliced zucchini and fennel on the barbecue. If you do not have access to a barbecue, use a cast-iron pan. All you are looking for is a thin layer of char.

In a large pot on the stove, heat the extra virgin olive oil. Sauté the onions and garlic for a few minutes until softened. Add the chili flakes and a pinch of salt and pepper. Add the charred zucchini, fennel, and chopped tomato. Stir and simmer for 6 to 8 minutes, allowing the vegetables to break down. Add the vegetable broth and increase the heat to high. Bring to a boil and then turn down to a simmer for 20 to 30 minutes. Add the red wine vinegar and another pinch of salt and pepper. Purée the soup with a blender or food processor. Check for seasoning and add more salt, pepper, and chili flakes if desired.

BLACK BEAN QUINOA BURGER

with coconut bacon and apple chutney

1 cup quinoa, cooked

1 cup black beans (fully cooked
    or from a can, rinsed and
    drained)

½ cup bread or panko crumbs

½ tsp smoked paprika

½ tsp chili powder

½ tsp cumin

1 tbsp BBQ sauce

1 tsp olive oil

½ medium white onion, diced

2 cloves garlic, minced

½ tsp salt

Chipotle BBQ Sauce

½ cup onion, finely chopped

2 cloves garlic, finely chopped

2 cups canned tomatoes

¼ cup fancy molasses

2 tbsp canned, smoked chipotle
    peppers

1 tsp cumin

1 tsp chili powder

1 tsp onion powder

1 tsp garlic powder

½ cup apple cider vinegar

1 cup brown sugar

¼ cup ketchup

Continued on next page

This vegan burger is easily customizable. We top it with coconut bacon, apple chutney, and all the other classic burger fixings. We encourage you to make it your own—it's sure to be mouthwatering any way you prepare it.

For the apple chutney, heat 1 tablespoon canola oil in a medium pot. Sauté the onions for 2 to 3 minutes, then add the spices and sauté for another minute. Add the rest of the ingredients and bring to a simmer, then turn down the heat to low, simmering for 1 to 2 hours while stirring occasionally. Cook until the grated apple is fully dissolved and the mixture has started to caramelize.

To make the BBQ sauce, first sauté onion and garlic in 2 tablespoons of canola oil. Add spices and cook for 2 to 3 minutes, then add the rest of the ingredients. Simmer for 1 hour. Blend until smooth. Add salt and pepper to taste.

Preheat the oven to 250°F. Whisk together all coconut bacon ingredients except the chipped coconut in a mixing bowl. Add the coconut and mix well, making sure that the coconut is evenly coated. Spread the coconut out on a parchment-lined baking sheet and bake for 20 to 30 minutes, stirring every 10 minutes until lightly browned and crispy.

To make the patties, chop the cooked black beans roughly and place them in a large mixing bowl with the rest of the ingredients. Use your hands to thoroughly mix and press together all the ingredients. Once fully mixed, form into patties, about 4 ounces each. Drizzle the patties with a little olive oil and a sprinkle of salt and pepper and grill for 4 to 5 minutes per side or bake at 375°F for 15 minutes.

From previous page

Coconut bacon
2 cups chipped coconut
1 tbsp canola oil
2 tbsp soy sauce or tamari
1 tbsp paprika
1 tbsp maple syrup
½ tsp liquid smoke (optional)
Salt and pepper to taste

Apple chutney
1 medium onion, diced
4 cups grated apple
¼ tsp ground coriander
¼ tsp ground cloves
¼ tsp ground cardamom
1 piece star anise
2 bay leaves
¼ tsp cinnamon
½ lemon
1 cup apple juice
¼ cup apple cider vinegar
¼ cup brown sugar
½ cup raisins
1 tbsp canola oil

To assemble
Lettuce leaves
Tomatoes, sliced
Red onion, sliced
Pickles
Avocado, smashed
BBQ sauce
6 burger buns

RASPBERRY TART

2 pints fresh raspberries

For the sweet pie dough
¾ cup unsalted butter
½ cup icing sugar
3½ cups all-purpose flour
1 egg
Pinch of salt

For the vanilla custard
2 cups whole milk
½ cup sugar
1 vanilla bean or 2 tsp pure
   vanilla extract
Pinch of salt
4 egg yolks
¼ cup cornstarch
2 tbsp butter

Our raspberries are in season for only a few weeks each summer. This raspberry tart recipe is delicious and a great way to showcase seasonal fruit.

Make the sweet pie dough. Cut the butter into small cubes and add to a mixing bowl. Add the rest of the dry ingredients and beat in a stand mixer with the paddle attachment until crumbly. If you are not using a stand mixer, rub the ingredients together in the bowl with your hands until the butter breaks up into smaller pieces and the mixture becomes crumbly. Add the egg and mix until a ball forms.

Press the dough into a disc shape, wrap tightly with plastic wrap, and refrigerate for at least 1 hour.

To prepare the tart shell, cut off small pieces of the sweet pie dough and press into a 9-inch tart mould, starting with the sides and working toward the middle. Press the dough in evenly and make sure there are no cracks. Chill the tart shell for 20 minutes before baking at 350°F for about 20 to 22 minutes.

Next, make the vanilla custard. In a medium saucepan, heat the milk and vanilla bean or vanilla extract over medium heat. Meanwhile, whisk together the egg yolks, cornstarch, and salt in a bowl until they are a creamy consistency. Stir the milk as it is heating to prevent it from burning on the bottom. Just before the milk comes to a boil, remove from the heat. Slowly pour the hot milk into the egg and sugar mixture while whisking vigorously.

Continued on page 75

From page 72

When the two mixtures are fully incorporated, transfer the liquid to the saucepan and return to the stovetop on medium heat. Whisk the custard consistently until it thickens, then remove from heat and transfer back to the mixing bowl. Whisk in the 2 tablespoons butter. Pour the custard into the cooked tart shell, leaving some room at the top for the raspberries (you may have pastry cream left over). Refrigerate the tart for at least 30 minutes.

To finish the tart, layer fresh raspberries on the tart. Sprinkle with icing sugar and serve with a dollop of fresh whipped cream.

FIREWEED JELLY

6 cups fireweed flowers

2 cups water

1 packet granulated pectin

2 cups white sugar

1 tbsp lemon juice
   (about ½ lemon)

Fireweed is abundant on the farm during the summer and makes for a beautifully coloured and delicious jelly. Bees also love harvesting nectar from the fireweed flowers.

In a medium saucepan, bring the fireweed flowers and water to a boil. Simmer for 2 to 3 minutes, then strain out the liquid. Place the liquid back in the pot, bringing it back up to a boil. Whisk in the pectin and then add the sugar, whisking thoroughly until dissolved. Simmer for 2 to 3 minutes. Add the lemon juice. The liquid should turn bright pink.

At this point, you can use a canning set-up to preserve the jelly by following the recommended steps. If you plan on using the jelly immediately, simply pour the liquid into a heatproof container and refrigerate overnight to let it set.

6 cups water
4 cups chopped rhubarb
1 cup sugar
2 lemons
4 Earl Grey tea bags

This iced tea recipe is a great way to use up your summer rhubarb harvest. It's simple, refreshing, and not too sweet.

Place the water, sugar, and chopped rhubarb in a large pot and bring to a boil. Simmer for 15 minutes. Take the pot off the heat and add the tea bags. Let steep 15 minutes. Strain the tea and squeeze 2 lemons into the mixture. Serve over ice.

FALL

FALL is a transitionary period on the farm. The frantic pace of summer starts to subside and the shorter, cooler days begin to slow the farm's productivity. Harvesting becomes the primary focus—rather than planting, cultivating, *and* harvesting, as it is for most of the summer. While the days get cooler, the ocean's buffering effect that we curse so much in the spring becomes a gift in the fall, often keeping our first frost at bay for many weeks after the equinox. This means harvesting can continue throughout October, November, and sometimes even early December.

To keep the flavours of our farm available all year long, the café team preserves as much as possible, freezing produce and bottling sauces, purées, and pickles. This is also our last opportunity to grab the last of the cultivated raspberries and wild blueberries that grow on the farm. As anyone who has picked berries knows, those who have patience and perseverance are justly rewarded for their efforts.

Fall is also wild mushroom season. Although we are fortunate enough to avail of cultivated mushrooms from several local suppliers all year long, in the fall foragers bring us beautiful chanterelles, hedgehogs (sweet tooth), and boletes. The complex flavours and textures of these mushrooms make them unlike anything you can buy in a grocery store. They are a true autumnal delight.

As the harvest slows, busyness at the farm slowly subsides. Tools and equipment are put away in storage; cover crops are cut and left to break down to add nutrients for the next season; and plastic is removed from the cold frames. With the busy season behind us at the café, there is time to try new recipes and to expand our baked goods to include more autumn flavours. While there is still much to do in the fall, there is a sense of relief in having completed another satisfying season.

WINTER STORAGE CROPS

One can't really farm in Newfoundland without having the old stalwarts in the field: cabbage, turnip, potatoes, and carrots. These crops have been grown in Newfoundland since its early days as a fishing port. Potatoes and carrots are remarkably easy to grow. For some reason, the soil in Newfoundland grows the sweetest carrots you'll find anywhere. Often crooked and bumpy from our rocky, shallow soil, they still grow well and taste just as sweet after months in cold storage as they did when we picked them. And our turnips are known to be some of the sweetest anyone has ever tasted.

Cabbage and turnip are generally straightforward to grow, but for the dreaded root maggot! These little monsters come from small housefly-looking insects that lay their eggs at the base of brassicas (the cabbage family, including turnips, broccoli, and radishes). When they hatch, they

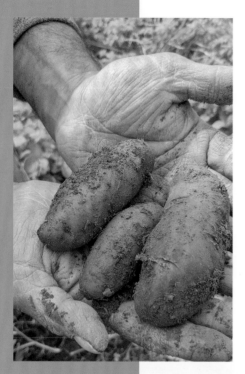

feed on the roots of these plants, cutting off their water and nutrient supply. The plant's growth is stunted and they fall over. Some survive but never fully recover. Once the bugs are in, they're in. The only way to keep them out is with a fine netting, preventing the fly from getting to the plants in the first place. We cover all our brassicas with netting from the time they are seeded or transplanted until they are harvested.

Rows of potatoes in flower are one of our favourite sights. The balls of purple, pink, and white are a sign that new potatoes are only a few weeks away. Potatoes planted in May are usually ready to harvest at the end of August. We use a 100-year-old, originally horse-drawn, potato digger to expose the tubers from their hills where they're picked by hand, sacked, and stored. We store our potatoes in the original farm cellar, where they keep perfectly all winter long.

FALL RECIPES

PICKLED FENNEL

1 head of fennel, sliced
1 tbsp salt

2 cups white vinegar
1 cup apple cider vinegar
1 cup water
¾ cup white sugar

Pickling spice
⅛ tsp peppercorns
1 to 2 bay leaves
½ tsp mustard seeds
⅛ tsp chili flakes
⅛ tsp fennel seeds

Fennel has a subtle licorice flavour that goes great with a sweet and acidic pickling brine. It's a great accompaniment to cheese plates, salads, or chicken. Use 1 tablespoon pre-mixed pickling spice or make your own.

Cut the fronds off the fennel (the wispy green herbs can be used in salad or to garnish a dish later), then cut the fennel bulb in half and then into 2- to 3-inch-long strips. Toss the fennel with 1 tablespoon salt and set aside.

Bring the vinegars, water, sugar, and pickling spice to a rolling boil.

Rinse the salt off the fennel and place it in Mason jars or a heatproof container. Pour the boiling pickling brine over the fennel. Set aside to cool. The pickle will keep, refrigerated, for up to a month.

For shelf-stable canning, follow the instructions listed on your canning set-up.

EGGPLANT AND CHANTERELLE PAN PIZZA

Pizza dough
3½ cups all-purpose flour
1 tbsp white sugar
2 tsp dry active yeast
2 tsp salt
1⅓ cups water,
   room temperature

Roasted garlic cream sauce
1 tbsp roasted garlic
1 shallot, minced
1 garlic clove, minced
1 tbsp unsalted butter
2 cups whipping cream
1 tsp apple cider vinegar
Pinch of cayenne
Salt and pepper

2 cups baby eggplants, halved
2 cups cleaned chanterelles,
   sliced
½ cup mozzarella cheese
2 tbsp extra virgin olive oil,
   plus extra for finishing

Eggplants and chanterelle mushrooms are great in combination with a creamy base to make an irresistible home-style pizza.

Mix the flour, sugar, and salt. Add the yeast and water and continue mixing for 8 to 10 minutes. Cover with plastic wrap and let rise for 30 minutes. Refrigerate overnight or use immediately.

For the garlic cream sauce: Cut a head of garlic in half and wrap in aluminum foil with a drizzle of olive oil. Roast at 350°F for 30 minutes. Heat the butter in a small saucepan and sauté the garlic and shallots on low heat. Add the cream and roasted garlic. Bring to a simmer and reduce by one-third. Season with the cayenne, salt, pepper, and cider vinegar. Set aside.

Preheat oven to 425°F.

Grease a 10-inch cast-iron pan with 2 tablespoons olive oil. If you do not have a large cast-iron pan, use a medium baking sheet. Roll out the pizza dough to fit the size of the pan. Place in the pan and gently stretch to fit to the sides. Cover and let the dough rise on top of the oven (or in another warm space) for 20 to 30 minutes.

Once the dough has risen, use your fingers to press down the dough and create a 1-inch crust around the edge. Spoon the garlic cream sauce inside the edges. Scatter the eggplant, chanterelles, and mozzarella over the pizza. Drizzle with a little more olive oil, sprinkle with salt and pepper, and bake for 15 to 20 minutes until golden.

WILD MUSHROOMS ON A BUTTERMILK BISCUIT

with purple bean salad

4 cups chanterelles, cleaned
2 tbsp unsalted butter
Salt and pepper
¼ cup white wine
2 tbsp chopped parsley

Purple bean salad
**4 cups purple runner beans,
   cleaned**
¼ cup aioli (page 130)
1 tbsp white vinegar
1 tsp white sugar
½ lemon, juiced
Salt and pepper

Buttermilk biscuits
4 cups all-purpose flour
½ tsp baking soda
2 tbsp baking powder
½ tsp salt
1 cup (½ lb) cold unsalted butter
2¼ cups buttermilk
Additional egg for egg wash

Wild mushrooms are one of our favourite ingredients when in season. If you aren't familiar with picking them yourself, you can find them at farmers' markets and even some grocery stores. You may substitute other runner beans for the purple beans.

Make the buttermilk biscuits: Use a cheese grater to grate the butter; place the grated butter in the freezer while you gather the rest of the ingredients (keeping the butter in the freezer helps prevent it from melting during the mixing stage). In a large bowl, mix the flour, baking soda, baking powder, and salt. Add the grated butter and rub together with your hands until the butter breaks up into small pea-sized bits. Add the buttermilk and fold together until just mixed. Try not to overmix the dough—the consistency should be a bit flaky. Cover the dough with a moist cloth and let rest for 10 minutes.

Preheat the oven to 375°F. On a well-floured work surface, roll out the biscuit dough to about 1 inch thick. Use a 3-inch round cookie cutter or a knife to cut the biscuits into 2-inch squares. Place the biscuits on a parchment-lined baking sheet. Mix 1 egg with 1 tablespoon water and whisk together to make an egg wash. Brush the top of each biscuit with the egg wash. Bake for about 20 minutes or until golden.

Continued on next page

From previous page

To make the bean salad, clean and trim the ends off the purple runner beans and cut into 1-inch batons. Mix the aioli with the vinegar, lemon juice, and salt. Toss the beans with the dressing and check for seasoning. Set aside.

Heat a large frying pan or cast-iron skillet on the stovetop. Place the mushrooms in the hot pan and toast them slightly, then deglaze with the white wine. Add 1 tablespoon butter and sauté the mushrooms until softened. Take off the heat, and stir in the remaining 1 tablespoon butter, the chopped parsley, and the salt and pepper to taste.

To plate, cut a warm buttermilk biscuit in half. Brush with butter and place the sautéed mushrooms on each half. Serve with a scoop of the purple bean salad.

BABY BEET SALAD
with ricotta and grilled shishito peppers

12 baby beets
8 to 10 shishito peppers
¼ cup red wine vinegar
¼ cup toasted pumpkin seeds
1 cup mustard greens or arugula
1 tbsp chopped fresh tarragon

Ricotta (purchased or
homemade using the recipe
on page 8)

Lemon vinaigrette
¼ cup lemon juice
1 tbsp cider vinegar
2 tbsp honey
1 clove garlic, chopped
1 shallot, diced
1 tsp Dijon mustard
1 cup canola oil
salt and pepper

Baby beets are a crowd pleaser, and the sweet beets pair nicely with the deep flavour and crunch of a grilled shishito pepper.

If you are making your own ricotta, do this first.

Place the baby beets in a large pot and cover with water. Add the red wine vinegar. Bring to a boil and then simmer for 30 minutes. Strain the beets. When cool enough to handle, peel the beets by rubbing off the skins. The skin should fall off easily while the beets are still warm.

Grill the shishito peppers on the barbecue or use a cast-iron skillet to char them. You don't need to fully cook them, just get some char on the outside, and allow them to soften slightly.

Whisk the lemon vinaigrette ingredients together; season to taste with salt and pepper. Leftover vinaigrette may be efrigerated for up to two weeks.

To prepare the salad, cut the beets into bite-sized wedges. Cut the shishito peppers into thick rings; the seeds are edible and not too spicy. Toss the beets, peppers, and mustard greens with 3 to 4 tablespoons of the lemon vinaigrette. Season with salt and pepper and more vinaigrette to taste. Place in a bowl and cover with chunks of fresh ricotta cheese, the toasted pumpkin seeds, and the chopped tarragon.

WARM FALL HARVEST SALAD

with roasted pumpkin, fall greens, and leek ash

1 small sugar pumpkin or
    winter squash
6 red Amarosa
    fingerling potatoes
1 fennel bulb
2 cups mustard greens
2 tbsp toasted almonds
1 leek
2 tbsp mascarpone cheese
Newfoundland sea salt

Kale juice (optional)
4 cups kale
2 apples

Vinaigrette
1 cup canola oil
½ cup balsamic vinegar
1 lemon, juiced
1 tbsp roasted garlic
1 tbsp Dijon mustard
¼ cup maple syrup
1 shallot, minced
Salt and pepper

Roast the vegetables: Preheat the oven to 350°F. Cut the pumpkin in half and remove the seeds. Drizzle with olive oil and season with salt and pepper. Place the halves flesh side down on a parchment-lined baking sheet. Toss the fingerling potatoes in olive oil and season with salt and pepper. Place them on the baking sheet with the pumpkin. Prepare the fennel by removing the fronds and cutting it in half. Drizzle with olive oil, season with salt and pepper, and wrap in aluminum foil. Roast the vegetables for 30 to 45 minutes until fork-tender.

To make the leek "ash," cut the top and bottom off the leek and discard. Cut the leek in half and wash thoroughly. Break apart the leek layers and lightly dry them with a paper towel, then place on a baking sheet and oven-roast until dark and crispy. Place in a blender or food processor and pulse until it becomes a fine powder resembling ashes. Place the ash in a small container and set aside. The leek ash adds depth and the bitterness will balance the sweet pumpkin.

To make the vinaigrette, place all ingredients in a bowl and whisk. Season to taste.

Juice the kale and apples together in an electric juicer.

To assemble the salad, cut the roasted vegetables and potatoes into bite-sized pieces. Warm them in the oven for a few minutes if necessary. Place a dollop of mascarpone cheese on the side of the plate. Toss the vegetables and greens with 1 tablespoon toasted almonds and 2 to 3 tablespoons of the vinaigrette. Arrange the warm salad around the mascarpone cheese. Top with the remainder of the toasted almonds. Add the optional kale juice and sprinkle with leek ash, more vinaigrette, and Newfoundland sea salt.

GNOCCHI WITH PEAS, CARAMELIZED ONIONS, AND BACON

Gnocchi
3 large russet potatoes
3 cups all-purpose flour
1 egg
1 tsp salt
Pinch of nutmeg (optional)
Pinch of white pepper (optional)

10 oz bacon, thick cut if possible
1½ cups fresh shucked
  English peas
½ cup whipping cream
½ cup vegetable or chicken stock
2 garlic cloves, minced
1 shallot, minced
1 tbsp olive oil
Pinch of chili flakes
½ lemon, juiced

1 cup pea shoots for garnish

Gnocchi is a comfort dish that is also fun to make. Here, we pair sweet fall peas with rich bacon lardons and bring it all together with a creamy sauce. Note: a potato ricer is essential to make the gnocchi from scratch.

Place the whole unpeeled russet potatoes in a large pot and cover with water. Add 1 tablespoon salt and bring to a boil. Boil for 20 to 25 minutes, while checking the potatoes for doneness with a fork. When the potato is fork-tender on the outside but slightly resistant in the centre, they are ready. If the potatoes are still hard all the way through, continue to boil while checking every few minutes.

While the potatoes are boiling, cut the bacon into ¼-inch strips and place in a large frying pan with 2 tablespoons water. Put the pan on medium-high heat until it starts to simmer. Stirring often, continue to cook the bacon until it starts to crisp. Strain off some of the fat halfway through and continue to cook until crispy. Strain and set aside.

Strain the potatoes and let them cool for a few minutes. Peel the potatoes and pass them through a potato ricer into a large mixing bowl. Add the flour, egg, and seasonings to the potato mixture and fold together by hand. Make sure that all the flour is incorporated; the dough should feel slightly firm. Try not to overwork the dough. Let the dough rest for 10 minutes.

Continued on next page

From previous page

Bring a large pot of lightly salted water to a boil. To form the gnocchi, cut off one-fourth of the dough and, on a lightly floured work surface, roll it into a long, even log about ½ inch thick. Cut the log into bite-sized pieces and set aside on a floured baking sheet. Repeat with the rest of the gnocchi dough. Boil the gnocchi for 2 to 3 minutes, until they float. Strain and set aside.

Heat 2 tablespoons olive oil in a large frying pan on medium-high heat. Add the minced shallots, garlic, and chili flakes and stir. Immediately add the chicken stock and whipping cream. Bring to a boil. Add the cooked gnocchi, peas, and bacon. Reduce to a simmer until the sauce thickens slightly. Add lemon juice and season with salt and pepper. Serve immediately and garnish with fresh pea shoots and a drizzle of olive oil.

TOMATO JAM

12 Roma tomatoes
½ cup white sugar
½ cup brown sugar
¼ cup red wine vinegar
½ tsp chili flakes
½ tsp ground coriander
½ tsp salt
½ tsp ground black pepper
1 bay leaf

Tomato jam is an easy way to use up a bounty of Roma tomatoes. It's a sweet and tangy condiment that goes great on a burger, with cheese and crackers, or with hummus.

Cut the tomatoes in half and scoop out the seeds, then roughly chop the flesh. Place all ingredients in a large pot and bring to a simmer. Reduce the heat to low and cook down for about 90 minutes, stirring occasionally. The jam should thicken and deepen in colour. Keep refrigerated for up to 2 weeks.

SQUASH RISOTTO
WITH SEARED KING OYSTER MUSHROOMS

1 cup arborio rice

**4 cups vegetable or
  chicken stock**

¼ cup white wine

1 shallot, minced

**1 buttercup squash or
  sugar pumpkin**

½ cup grated Parmesan

2 to 3 king oyster mushrooms

½ lemon, juiced

2 tbsp olive oil

2 tbsp salted butter

1 tbsp fresh thyme leaves

2 tbsp pine nuts

We prepare this comforting risotto dish with king oyster mushrooms produced by our neighbours in Portugal Cove. The king oysters resemble a scallop in flavour and texture and pair very nicely with sweet fall squash.

Preheat the oven to 350°F. Prepare the squash by washing it and cutting it in half, then removing the seeds. Drizzle each half with olive oil, and season with salt and pepper. Wrap the halves in aluminum foil and oven-roast for 45 minutes or until fork-tender.

While the squash is roasting, prepare the mushrooms by slicing them into discs that resemble the size of a scallop, then score each side of the mushroom with a knife in a criss-cross pattern. Set aside.

When the squash is fully cooked, allow to cool for a few minutes. Scoop out the flesh and place in a bowl. Smash it with a fork or a whisk to create a smooth purée-like texture.

To prepare the risotto, heat the vegetable or chicken stock in a large saucepan. Add 2 tablespoons olive oil to a separate large frying pan. Sauté the shallot for a few seconds and then add the arborio rice. Stir the rice until it is evenly coated in the olive oil and continue to cook for 2 to 3 minutes, until the rice starts to toast. Toasting the rice allows it to absorb the liquid we are about to add and deepens the flavour of the risotto. Deglaze the pan with the white wine. When the liquid reduces by half, begin to add chicken stock, one ladleful or ½ cup at a time,

Continued on page 113

From page 110

just enough to cover the rice and simmer—you do not want to drown the rice. Add the squash purée and mix thoroughly. Continue to stir. When the rice absorbs the stock, add another ladleful before it becomes dry. Repeat this process of adding stock until the rice is cooked but slightly al dente. At this point, it should be fairly creamy and somewhat loose but not runny. Stir in the Parmesan, butter, half of the fresh thyme leaves, and season with salt and pepper.

Sauté the mushrooms in a frying pan with lots of butter—about 2 minutes per side or until golden. Season the mushrooms generously with salt, pepper, and lemon juice. Serve the risotto topped with the seared mushrooms and finish it with the rest of the fresh thyme leaves, more grated Parmesan, and a drizzle of olive oil.

BLUEBERRY CHEESECAKE BARS

Crust
4 cups rolled oats
¾ cup brown sugar
¼ cup honey
2 tsp cinnamon
½ tsp salt
⅓ cup coconut oil
½ cup melted unsalted butter

Batter
4 cups cream cheese, softened
4 eggs
1 tsp vanilla
1 cup + 3 tbsp white sugar
2 cups blueberries,
 fresh or frozen

Blueberry compote
2 cups blueberries,
 fresh or frozen
¼ cup white sugar
Zest of 1 lemon

We love making cheesecake bars because they are a bit quicker to bake than a full classic cheesecake and easier to portion and serve. This recipe uses a gluten-free crust for the bar, similar to a graham crumb.

Preheat the oven to 350°F and mix the rolled oats with the sugar, honey, cinnamon, salt, and coconut oil (save the melted butter for later). Spread the oat mixture on a baking sheet and bake for 20 to 30 minutes, stirring occasionally, until golden. While the oats are baking, take the cream cheese out of the refrigerator to soften. Once the oats are nicely toasted, allow them to cool for a few minutes and pulse in a food processor or blender until they break up into small pieces. Mix the oat pieces with the melted butter. In a lightly greased 9 by 13-inch baking dish, press the crust mixture to fit to the edges of the dish. The crust should be about ¼ inch thick. Set aside any excess crust mixture.

To make the cheesecake batter, mix the cream cheese, eggs, and sugar in a food processor or stand mixer until creamy and smooth. Combine 2 cups blueberries with the batter and pour over the crust. Bake for 15 to 20 minutes at 325°F.

While the cheesecake is baking, make a blueberry compote by heating 2 cups blueberries with ¼ cup sugar and the lemon zest. Simmer for 15 to 20 minutes and set aside to cool.

Allow the cheesecake bars to cool completely before serving. Slice and serve with a tablespoon of blueberry compote.

PIN CHERRY CRULLERS

Choux paste
¾ cup water
¾ cup whole milk
½ cup + 2 tbsp unsalted butter
½ tbsp white sugar
½ tsp salt
1½ cups all-purpose flour
5 eggs

Pin cherry glaze
1 cup pin cherries
1 tbsp white sugar
1½ cups icing sugar
1 tbsp melted butter

2 to 3 cups canola oil for frying

Homemade cruller donuts are irresistible. We use a classic choux paste as the base and pipe it out using a special tip to form the crullers. In this recipe, we top them with a sweet and tart glaze made from fresh pin cherries.

To make the choux paste, place the water, milk, butter, sugar, and salt in a medium saucepan. Bring to a simmer. Add the flour and stir vigorously with a wooden spoon for 2 to 3 minutes. When you see a thin film coat the bottom of the pan, transfer the paste to a stand mixer fitted with a paddle attachment. Mix the choux paste on high for 2 minutes and then add the eggs, one at a time, waiting until each egg is incorporated before adding the next. Continue mixing on high speed for 3 to 4 minutes. The choux paste should be smooth and shiny. Transfer to a piping bag fitted with a large star piping tip. Wrap the piping bag in plastic wrap and refrigerate for 20 minutes.

While the choux paste is chilling, heat the canola oil in a large pot. Monitor the temperature with a thermometer and try to keep it around 350°F.

Heat the pin cherries with 1 tablespoon sugar in a small saucepan. Simmer for 5 minutes and then strain through a fine-mesh sieve. Mix 3 tablespoons pin cherry juice with 1½ cups icing sugar and 1 tablespoon melted butter. Whisk until completely incorporated. If the glaze is too loose, or too tight, add more icing sugar or cherry juice accordingly.

Continued on page 118

From page 116

Prepare to make the crullers by cutting out 12 3-inch-square pieces of parchment paper. Pipe out a double layered ring of choux paste onto each parchment piece. Carefully transfer the crullers to the hot oil, choux paste side down. The parchment paper should naturally fall off after a minute or two and you can remove it with tongs. Fry the cruller for 2 minutes on the first side, then flip it fry for another minute. Fry 2 to 3 crullers at a time, depending on the pot size. Place the finished crullers on a baking sheet lined with paper towel.

Let the crullers cool for a few minutes before dipping them in the cherry glaze.

DOLGO APPLE FIZZ

Syrup
2 lbs Dolgo apples
4 cups water
4 cups white sugar

For two beverages
16 oz carbonated water
3 oz brandy
Lemon peel
Ice

Dolgo apples have a vibrant bright red skin that carries over into the syrup we make from them, giving the drink a nice pink hue.

Wash the Dolgo apples, remove the stems, and cut them in half. Place them in a large pot with the water and sugar and bring to a simmer. Cook until the mixture becomes a pulp, about 10 minutes, and then strain through a fine-mesh sieve. Discard the pulp. Set the syrup aside to cool.

For each beverage, fill a glass with ice, pour in 3 ounces Dolgo syrup and 1 1/2 ounces brandy, and top it up with roughly 8 ounces carbonated water. Garnish with lemon zest.

APPLE BUTTER

12 apples (crabapples or
   Granny Smith)
1 lemon, halved
2 cinnamon sticks
4 cloves
2 star anise
1 cup brown sugar
2 cups apple cider vinegar
Salt

Apple butter is a winter pantry staple that can be spread on toast or used on a cheese plate or as a layer in a cake. It is particularly good in a ginger cake.

Remove the apple stems and cores. Cut the apple pieces into wedges. Place in a large pot with the rest of the ingredients and set to medium heat. Cook until the apples are softened. Turn the heat to low and simmer 2 to 3 hours while stirring occasionally, being sure to scrape down to the bottom. Look for a deep caramelization of the apples: they will turn a rich brown.

After the apple butter has reduced and caramelized, strain through a fine-mesh sieve into a container. Use a hand blender to ensure a smooth consistency. The apple butter can be refrigerated for a month or canned for longer preservation.

WINTER

W HEN the dark days of winter arrive, a collective sigh goes out across the farm. The greenhouses and fields are put to bed and growers, farmers, and chefs take a well-earned rest.

During the winter, we work on projects that we can never find time for during the busy season. We fill our days by building or refinishing benches and tables for the café or working on rug hookings to adorn the café's walls.

But not all is quiet during the post-solstice season. Fierce nor'easter storms make their way up the Atlantic coast, bringing punishing winds and smothering loads of snow. Greenhouses and equipment must be latched down and winterized to prevent damage. Inside, we prepare by keeping a hefty supply of firewood on hand, along with plenty of vegetables and preserves stored in our root cellar. Usually filled with beets, carrots, turnip, kohlrabi, and cabbage, the root cellar provides year-round access to vegetables for the café and our home kitchens.

Hearty root-vegetable dishes fill the belly and warm the soul. Jams, pickles, and other preserves provide a potent punch of spring and summer flavours even on the coldest of day. Microgreens, which we grow and harvest on light shelves in the café, are another taste of spring. As garnishes on soups and savoury baked goods, these shoots provide the crisp fresh flavour of peas, corn, basil, or radish and remind us that spring will return.

During the holiday season, we shut down the café and garden centre for two weeks so that we can spend quality time tucked away with family and friends. That doesn't mean our bakers are giving their rolling pins and ovens a rest—they produce Christmas cookies, cakes, and pies to treat visitors.

Winter continues and eventually we turn our sights to the growing season ahead. We begin our production plans and order seeds and supplies. We review the year gone by, the crops that did well and those that did not, and we talk with farmers and chefs about which vegetables and herbs might be featured in the upcoming season's menu. While the darkest season in Newfoundland can be long and harsh, winter doesn't last forever and it's never long until the first shoots are pushing through the soil.

WINTER GREENS

There is nothing quite like fresh greens picked from the greenhouse in the middle of January. Growing vegetables through the winter in Newfoundland without sophisticated greenhouses and expensive heating and lighting systems seems an impossible task—but the fact is, anyone can grow fresh greens and more with a simple, but sturdy, cold frame.

We seed greens at the beginning of September and harvest them through the winter. The secret is to bury half of your greenhouse in the earth to shelter it, insulate the northern wall, or use supplemental heat when temperatures dip below -15°C overnight. The inside of our greenhouse has dropped to -10°C and at that temperature, spinach, arugula, and mizuna will look frozen, but a bit of sun or bright cloud will warm the greenhouse the next day and they spring right back.

We also grow microgreens in the café through the winter. Pea seeds soaked overnight and planted in a small container of potting soil give fresh greens for sandwiches or salads. They taste just like fresh peas! Try sunflower seeds or, for more of a challenge, radish and other brassica seeds for a spicy kick.

THE ROOT CELLAR

The first Murrays to settle in Portugal Cove (circa 1820) must have worked relentlessly to build shelters to protect themselves and their provisions from the harsh New-foundland weather. The nearly 200-square-foot subterra-nean cellar attached to our family's ancestral home bears witness to meeting that challenge.

The root cellar was excavated out of the side of a steep bank across from Murray's Pond. The cellar has been in continuous use ever since; it is currently a holding area for the café's root vegetables harvested from our vegetable farm. The cellar has often been filled with potatoes, carrots, turnip, cabbage, and parsnips. In the past, it was used to chill milk and hang and cure sides of lamb, pork, and beef. Storage shelves for pickles, jams, and bottled rabbit, seal, and moose were constructed just inside the door. The small passageway into the cellar is about 3 feet wide; small wooden barrels of pickled pork and beef lined the opposite alcove, and bundles of salt fish and kippers hung from the ceiling.

The large stones used to construct the cellar were gathered as the farmland was cleared and stacked in cross-joint rows mortared together with a primitive cement made of wood ash, grey gravel, and straw. The base course of stones are large, square-set stones chiselled to fit. A number of dead men stones protrude to the wall's outside edge, offering stability and strength to the stacked wall stones. The walls are between 3 and 4 feet thick, with smaller hand-picked stones packed along the outside of the wall to facilitate drainage. The earthen floor has rough sawn boards spaced roughly 1 inch on centre, then nailed to 2-inch-diameter spruce-stick floor joists. This rough floor facilitates air circulation and helps keep temperatures and humidity consistent throughout. The earthen floor regulates moisture levels and provides drainage during heavy rainfalls, spring thaw, and runoff.

The most marvellous part of our cellar is the small doorway—about 50 inches high by 20 inches wide—that leads from the cellar into the porch of the house. This door provided access to the vegetables, meat, and other stored provisions from the kitchen with no need to go outside.

The smells that came from the cellar throughout the season were amazing. The sweet smell of carrots, parsnips, and cabbage mixed with salt fish and earthen floor greeted you on cold winter days. And the pungent smells of decaying potatoes and mummified carrots assailed your nostrils as you cleaned up the cellar in June and made ready for the fall harvest.

Our family business still uses our root cellar today. We owe a substantial debt to our Murray ancestors for having the forbearance and energy to build and maintain this marvellous structure that has served us well for over 200 years.

WINTER RECIPES

BEET FRITES WITH GARLIC AIOLI

6 medium beets
2 tbsp vegetable oil
½ cup water
Salt and pepper
1 cup cornstarch or potato starch
3 cups canola oil for frying

Garlic aioli
1 cup mayonnaise
1 tbsp olive oil
½ tsp Dijon mustard
1 egg yolk
1 head of garlic
½ lemon, juice and zest
½ tsp apple cider vinegar
Salt and pepper

Beet frites (or beet fries) are a crispy, salty, and sweet crave-worthy snack that also works well as an appetizer or side dish.

Mix the garlic aioli ingredients in a bowl and season to taste. The aioli can be made ahead of time; it can be refrigerated for a week.

Preheat oven to 400°F.

Trim stems and greens from the beets. Rinse the beets, place them in a large bowl, and toss with the 2 tablespoons vegetable oil and a generous pinch of salt and pepper.

Place the beets and water in a parchment-lined roasting pan. Cover tightly with aluminum foil. Roast 45 minutes to 1 hour, or until tender. Check the doneness of the beets by poking them with a knife. When the knife easily slides into the centre of the beet, they are ready. The beets can be roasted a day in advance to save time.

Allow the beets to cool. Peel and cut into French-fry shapes, cubes, or wedges. Place the cut beets in a mixing bowl with the cornstarch and toss thoroughly to coat—this will help them get beautifully crispy on the outside. Remove the coated beets from the remaining cornstarch and set aside.

To fry the beets, heat 3 cups oil to 350°F in a large flat-bottomed pan on the stovetop. Carefully fry the beets in three to four small batches for a few minutes for each batch. When they are crispy, scoop out with tongs and place them on a paper towel to drain. Sprinkle with a little more salt. Serve while hot with a dollop of garlic aioli and a slice of lemon.

SHAVED KOHLRABI SALAD

with apple, bacon, thyme, and apple cider vinaigrette

1 large kohlrabi
1 Granny Smith apple
4 slices bacon
Fresh thyme sprigs
Olive oil

Vinaigrette
⅓ cup apple cider vinegar
Juice of ½ lemon
½ tsp Dijon mustard
1 tbsp honey or maple syrup
1 garlic clove, minced
1 shallot, finely diced
Pinch of chili flakes
1 cup canola oil
Pinch of salt and pepper

Thinly shaved raw kohlrabi has a similar taste and texture to that of the heart of romaine lettuce: sweet, crunchy, and amazingly fresh. It works well as a neutral base for this salad. In the fall, we used crabapples to make cider and ended up with a large batch of apple cider vinegar after a batch went sour. The tartness of the apple cider vinaigrette is a great match for the sweetness of kohlrabi and the saltiness of the bacon.

Use a knife to cut off the top and bottom of the kohlrabi bulb, then cut it in half from top to bottom. Use a vegetable peeler to remove the remaining green outer layer of the kohlrabi, then slice it into 1-inch-thick half moons. Use a vegetable peeler to make ribbons of the flesh and place them in a bowl with cold water and set aside.

Dice the bacon and place in a frying pan with 2 to 3 tablespoons water. Use medium heat to render the fat and make crispy bacon bits. Strain on a paper towel and set aside.

Remove the leaves from the thyme sprigs and set aside.

Make the vinaigrette: Whisk all ingredients together in a bowl and season to taste. Refrigerate in an airtight container for up to a month.

To prepare the salad, toss together the drained kohlrabi, thinly sliced Granny Smith apple, bacon bits, thyme sprigs, and some of the vinaigrette. Check the seasoning and add more salt or vinaigrette as needed.

Finish the salad with more bacon bits and thyme leaves on top and a drizzle of olive oil.

ROASTED FENNEL AND KOHLRABI SOUP WITH PRESERVED LEMON AND GREMOLATA

3 fennel bulbs

1 large kohlrabi

1 medium onion

3 garlic cloves

2 tbsp diced preserved lemon
   or 1 fresh lemon

Pinch of chili flakes

4 cups vegetable or
   chicken broth

4 tbsp + 2 tsp canola oil

Gremolata

1 cup parsley

2 garlic cloves

1 lemon, juice and zest

½ cup olive oil

Pinch of chili flakes

Salt and pepper

Roasted fennel adds a wonderful aroma to this puréed winter soup. It's fairly easy to prepare, and the gremolata gives a colourful pop that ties everything together. We use preserved lemon but fresh lemon works just as well.

To roast the fennel, preheat the oven to 375°F. Cut the fennel in half, drizzle with a little olive oil, and add a pinch of salt and pepper. Loosely wrap in aluminum foil and place in a roasting pan. Roast for 30 to 40 minutes or until the fennel is completely soft and beginning to caramelize.

Peel and dice the kohlrabi. Slice the onions and garlic. Prepare the preserved lemon by cutting out the pith and slicing the skin into small strips. If you're using fresh lemon, juice and zest 1 lemon.

In a soup pot, heat the canola oil over medium heat. Add the onions and garlic and sauté until translucent. Add the diced kohlrabi and roasted fennel, season with a pinch of salt and pepper, and continue to sauté for 5 to 8 minutes, until the kohlrabi begins to soften. Add the broth and bring to a simmer. Continue to simmer for 20 minutes or until the kohlrabi is completely fork-tender.

Purée the soup with the lemon and chili flakes using a hand-held or jug blender in small batches. Keep warm in a pot until ready to serve.

To make the gremolata, finely chop all ingredients, mix with the olive oil, season to taste, and keep refrigerated in an airtight container for up to 2 weeks.

SHAKSHUKA

3 tbsp olive oil
½ medium onion, diced
1 green pepper, diced
1 jalapeno, diced
1 cayenne pepper, diced
2 cloves garlic
1 28 oz (796 ml) can diced
   tomatoes or 6 large fresh
   picked tomatoes, diced
1 tsp ground cumin
1 tsp chili powder
2 tsp paprika
Salt
Pepper

4 eggs
Feta cheese
Herb mixture (parsley, oregano,
   mint, chives, or other available
   fresh herbs)
Bread

Shakshuka is a seasonal brunch staple at The Grounds. A spiced tomato and pepper sauce is used to poach the eggs. The dish is finished with cheese and herbs and served with grilled bread or toast.

Heat the olive oil in a medium saucepan on medium heat. Add the onions and sauté for 2 minutes while stirring. Add the diced peppers and garlic and continue to sauté the pepper and onion mixture for 2 to 3 minutes. Add spices and stir and sauté for another 2 minutes. Finally, add the diced tomato and season generously with salt and pepper. Stir well and bring to a simmer, then reduce the heat to low and continue to simmer for 20 to 30 minutes.

While the sauce is cooking, prepare the herb mixture by finely chopping the parsley, oregano, mint, and chives. We use whatever fresh herbs we have available for the mixture, but it always starts with fresh chopped parsley.

When the sauce has simmered for 20 to 30 minutes and turned a deep red, remove from the heat and check the seasoning. Add more salt, pepper, or spices to taste.

Transfer a few ladlefuls of the tomato sauce to a shallow saucepan that has a lid. Heat the sauce on medium low and use a spoon to create four wells. Crack 1 egg into each well. Sprinkle crumbled feta cheese on the sauce and eggs. Cover and simmer for 3 minutes. Prepare the toast or grilled bread while the eggs are poaching. Remove the lid and check for a soft to medium poached egg. You can cook it for longer if you prefer solid yolks.

Top with fresh chopped herbs and serve with toast.

COFFEE-ROASTED BEET TARTINE
with nettle pesto and ricotta

1 loaf of country bread
6 medium beets
2 cups used coffee grounds
1 tbsp salt
¼ cup olive oil
½ cup ricotta, store-bought
  or homemade (page 8)
Zest and juice of 1 lemon
1 tbsp honey

Nettle pesto
3 garlic cloves
2 tbsp toasted almonds
2 tbsp Parmesan cheese, grated
⅔ cup blanched nettles
Salt
4 tbsp olive oil

Using a mixture of freshly used coffee grounds and salt to coat the beets before roasting complements their natural sweetness and brings depth to this delicious open-faced sandwich. Used coffee grounds should be refrigerated in a sealed container until ready to use.

The nettle pesto is a vibrant addition—we make and freeze large batches of it in the spring while the wild, herbaceous stinging nettle bushes are abundant in the ditches and crevices surrounding some of our vegetable patches.

Preheat the oven to 375°F. Remove the beet stems and greens if they are still attached and set aside. Rinse the beets with warm water, drain, and toss in a large mixing bowl with the coffee grounds, 1 tablespoon salt, and ¼ cup oil. Place in a parchment-lined roasting pan and cover with aluminum foil. Roast until fork-tender—about 45 minutes, depending on the size of the beet.

After roasting, let the beets cool, and brush off the coffee-salt mixture. Peel the beets and slice into thin discs. Set aside.

To make the nettle pesto, first carefully blanch the stinging nettles in lightly salted boiling water for 30 seconds, using tongs or gloves to handle the nettles. Transfer to an ice bath, then drain. Roughly chop and set aside.

In a food processor, blend the garlic and almonds until coarsely chopped. Add the grated Parmesan, then the nettles and salt. Drizzle in the olive oil 1 tablespoon at a time, until the mixture reaches the desired consistency.

In a small mixing bowl, mix the ricotta with the lemon juice, zest, and 1 teaspoon honey.

To assemble the tartine, spread the ricotta on a slice of country loaf. Neatly place the sliced coffee-roasted beets on the ricotta and finish by generously drizzling the nettle pesto over the beets.

LOADED POTATO SALAD

with pickled garlic scapes, pickled chanterelles, and bacon

6 to 8 medium, white-fleshed
  waxy potatoes
½ cup garlic aioli (page 130)
1 tsp Dijon mustard
6 strips bacon
½ cup pickled chanterelles
½ cup pickled garlic scapes
2 tbsp chopped fresh parsley
  or chives
Salt and pepper to taste

In this side dish, we add local ingredients to elevate the classic and sometimes overlooked potato salad. Here, we use our preserves from the summer and fall. At home, you can use whatever pickled or fermented vegetables you have on hand—other additions that we love to use are pickled wild hops, pickled baby onions or carrots, pickled shishito peppers, or cucumber pickles. The idea is to adapt and use ingredients that are easily available to you.

Rinse the potatoes in warm water. Dice the potatoes into 1-inch cubes—we leave the skin on—and place in a large pot. Cover with lightly salted water. Bring to a boil and reduce the heat to medium. Cook until fork-tender but not mushy. Strain and let cool completely.

Dice the bacon and render out the fat in a frying pan on medium heat until crispy. Drain the bacon bits on a paper towel and set aside.

Dice the pickled ingredients.

Combine the cooked potatoes, garlic aioli, and Dijon mustard in a large bowl. Mix in half of the bacon bits, pickles, and herbs. Season with salt and pepper to taste. Transfer to a serving dish and sprinkle the remaining bacon bits, pickles, and herbs on top.

CUBAN-STYLE CALZONE
WITH PICKLES AND DIJONNAISE DIPPER

Calzone dough

3½ cups all-purpose flour

1 tbsp white sugar

2 tsp dry active yeast

2 tsp salt

1⅓ cups water,
room temperature

Braised pork

2.2 lbs pork shoulder

2 cups water

2 cups orange juice

1 head of garlic, halved

1 tsp ground cumin

Dijonnaise dipper

1 cup garlic aioli (page 130)

⅓ cup Dijon mustard

Salt and pepper

Per calzone

½ cup (125 g) calzone dough

1 slice of black forest ham

¼ cup braised pork

2 tbsp chopped dill pickles

¼ cup grated Swiss cheese

1 tsp olive oil

The dough in this recipe is versatile and forgiving. The crust is crispy and chewy, and the filling bakes together inside to create the perfect melty bite. Both the pork and the dough can be prepared a day ahead.

Place the ingredients for the braised pork in a braising pan or slow cooker. Cover and bake at 325°F for 4 hours, or on high heat in a slow cooker for 5 to 6 hours. The meat is ready when it is fork-tender. Strain off most of the liquid and shred the pork with a fork. Season generously with salt and pepper.

Mix the flour, sugar, and salt. Add the yeast and water and continue mixing for 8 to 10 minutes. Cover with plastic wrap and let rise for 30 minutes. Refrigerate overnight or use immediately.

When you are ready to assemble the calzones, preheat the oven to 450°F.

On a lightly floured countertop, divide the calzone dough into six balls and let rise for 10 minutes. Generously cover one dough ball and work surface with flour. Roll into a flat oval, about the size of two fists and ¼ inch thick. Place a slice of ham in the centre of the flattened dough, then top with ¼ cup shredded braised pork, pickles, and grated Swiss cheese. Fold the dough over to create a pocket and pinch down the edges. Fold about ½ inch of the edge back and pinch it down to create a crust. Repeat with the remaining dough balls. Place calzones on a parchment-lined baking sheet and let rest for 20 minutes.

Drizzle with olive oil and bake 15 minutes until golden.

BBQ PARSNIP AND POTATO FLATBREAD

with smoked cheddar and pickled red onions

2 to 3 large parsnips
2 Russet potatoes
½ cup grated smoked cheddar
½ cup BBQ sauce (recipe page 69)
2 cups white vinegar
½ cup white sugar

Flatbread
2½ cups all-purpose flour
1 tsp salt
¼ cup vegetable shortening
⅔ cup water, room temperature

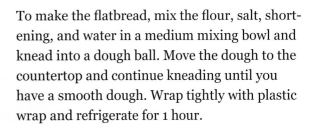

Shredded parsnip tossed in BBQ sauce and roasted has a similar flavour and texture to that of pulled pork and is especially delicious on flatbreads or pizza. This is a fun afternoon project if you want to make the flatbreads yourself, or you can substitute store-bought naan bread. Flatbreads can be made ahead and stored in a container in the refrigerator for a few days.

To make the flatbread, mix the flour, salt, shortening, and water in a medium mixing bowl and knead into a dough ball. Move the dough to the countertop and continue kneading until you have a smooth dough. Wrap tightly with plastic wrap and refrigerate for 1 hour.

After chilling, split the dough ball into four equal pieces and pat each piece into flat spheres. Using a rolling pin and a generous amount of flour, roll each flatbread out into a thin circle or oval, making sure that it fits your largest flat-bottomed frying pan. Alternatively, use a pizza stone to cook the flatbreads.

Heat the frying pan on medium heat and place one flatbread at a time in the pan, cooking 2 to 3 minutes on each side. When the dough starts to puff up, it is ready to flip. Wipe out any residual flour from the pan after each flatbread.

Peel and slice the onion into thin strips. Boil the vinegar and sugar, add the onions, and remove from the heat immediately. Make sure that the onions are fully submerged, and allow to cool fully.

Preheat the oven to 350°F. Rinse the parsnips under warm water and cut off the tip and tail. Use a cheese grater or food processor to shred the parsnips. Toss the shredded parsnips with the BBQ sauce in a mixing bowl. Move parsnips to a baking sheet and roast for 15 to 20 minutes until lightly caramelized.

Continued on next page

From previous page

Place the whole potatoes in a saucepan of lightly salted water. Bring to a boil and boil for 5 minutes, take off the heat, and let sit 10 minutes. The potatoes should be about half cooked—soft on the outside but still slightly hard in the middle. Test with a fork. Strain and cool the par-cooked potatoes, slice into thin discs, and set aside.

To assemble the flatbreads, first spread on some BBQ sauce as a base. Layer the sliced potatoes on top, and then add the BBQ parsnip. Cover with cheese, drizzle with olive oil, and sprinkle with salt and pepper. Bake at 350°F for 10 to 12 minutes.

Slice into five or six pieces. Finish with pickled onions. Pickled jalapenos or hot sauce are great additions if you want to bring up the heat.

MAPLE-ROASTED CARROTS WITH LIME ZEST, YOGURT, AND ROASTED PEANUTS

4 to 6 medium carrots
¼ cup amber maple syrup
2 tbsp unsalted butter
2 tbsp olive oil
2 limes
2 tbsp Greek yogurt
½ tsp ground cumin
¼ tsp cayenne
Salt and pepper
½ cup peanuts,
   roasted and crushed

Carrots are a great vessel for this combination of sweet, salty, sour, and spicy garnishes. In this recipe, the carrots are first roasted to begin the cooking process, and then finished in a frying pan to add extra flavour.

Preheat the oven to 375°F. Peel and wash the carrots. Toss in the salt, pepper, olive oil, and half of the maple syrup. Spread out on a baking sheet and roast for 15 to 20 minutes.

Transfer the roasted carrots to a large frying pan with the butter, the rest of the maple syrup, and the spices. Season with a little salt and pepper. On medium-low heat, sauté the carrots until the maple syrup begins to caramelize and the edges of the carrots start to brown.

Transfer to a serving platter. Drizzle with yogurt and sprinkle with cilantro and peanuts.

CHICKPEA, FETA, AND KALE HAND PIE

1 recipe pie dough (see page 18)

Filling
1 can (19 oz / 540 ml) chickpeas,
**   drained and rinsed**
1 cup feta cheese, crumbled
1 large bunch of kale, chopped
1 medium onion, chopped
3 cloves garlic, minced
Chili flakes
Zest and juice of 1 lemon
2 tbsp unsalted butter
Salt and pepper

1 egg + 1 tbsp water or milk
**   for egg wash**

A rustic vegetarian pastry.

To make the filling, sauté the onion, garlic, and chili flakes (to taste) with the butter until softened. Add the kale and continue to cook until it is wilted. Add the chickpeas and cook for another 5 minutes. Fold in the feta, lemon juice, and zest. Season with salt and pepper.

Roll out the pie dough to ⅛ inch thick. Use a 3-inch ring cutter (or the top of a glass or a small bowl) to cut out circles of dough. Cut out eight circles, re-rolling the dough if necessary.

Take one circle of dough to use as the base of your hand pie. Lightly brush with the egg wash. Spoon 2 tablespoons filling into the centre, leaving space around the edge, then place another circle of dough over the top over and press down around the edges. Poke a hole in the top and crimp the edges with a fork. Continue with the other dough circles.

In a small bowl, whisk together the egg with 1 tablespoon water or milk to make an egg wash. Brush dough with the egg wash. Bake at 400°F for 15 minutes.

CURRIED POTATO AND ROOT-VEGETABLE SAMOSA WITH ONION CHUTNEY

1 recipe pie dough (see page 18)

4 cups diced potatoes (3 potatoes)
1 cup diced turnip (½ turnip)
1 cup diced carrot (1 large carrot)
2 cups diced parsnip (1 parsnip)
2 tbsp canola oil
1 medium onion, diced
3 cloves garlic, diced
1 tbsp garam masala
1 tbsp curry powder
1 tsp ground cumin
½ tsp cayenne
2 cups vegetable broth or water
½ cup chopped cilantro
1 lime, zested and juiced
Salt and pepper

Make the pie crust using the method on page 18.

Boil the potatoes in lightly salted water until softened. Strain and let cool.

Place a large sauté pan over medium heat. Add the canola oil, onions, garlic, and spices. Simmer until translucent. Add the diced turnip, carrot, and parsnip. Simmer for a few minutes until the vegetables start to soften. Add the broth and simmer until the vegetables are cooked through and the broth reduces to a paste-like consistency. Season generously with salt and pepper and let cool. Fold the cooked potatoes into the vegetable curry mixture. Mix in the chopped cilantro, lime juice, and zest, and check for seasoning.

To assemble the samosas, roll the dough into a large rectangle, about ¼ inch thick. Cut into six squares. Place ¼ cup filling in each dough square and brush the edges with a little water. Fold the dough over into a triangle and crimp the edges with a fork. Refrigerate for 20 minutes.

Bake at 375°F for 15 to 20 minutes or until golden.

BROWN BUTTER CHOCOLATE CHIP COOKIES

1 cup unsalted butter, cubed

1⅔ cups brown sugar

2 eggs

1 tsp vanilla

1 tsp baking soda

½ tsp baking powder

1 tsp salt

3¼ cups flour

1½ cups chocolate chips

Optional: 1 cup chopped pecans

The brown butter in this recipe gives a rich, nutty flavour to the cookies.

To make the brown butter, gently simmer the cubed butter in a pan over medium heat for 10 to 15 minutes while whisking occasionally. The milk solids will start to caramelize and release a nutty smell; at this point, carefully take the butter off the heat and pour it into a heatproof bowl. Let cool to room temperature.

Place the room-temperature brown butter in the bowl of an electric mixer with the paddle attachment. Add the brown sugar and cream together until light, fluffy, and doubled in volume. Add the eggs and vanilla and mix.

Combine the dry ingredients and add to the butter mixture. Combine well. Finally, add the chocolate chips.

Scoop out hunks of dough (we weigh our cookies out to 100 g) onto a parchment-lined baking sheet. Refrigerate for about 20 minutes before baking at 340°F for 12 minutes.

CHAGA CHAI TEA LATTE

1 small (thumb size) chunk
  of chaga
3 cardamom pods
1 tsp ground allspice
1 tsp whole cloves
1 thumb of fresh ginger
2 cinnamon sticks
8 peppercorns
8 cups water
2 cups milk (dairy or
  dairy alternative)
2 tsp white sugar
2 chai tea bags

This is a warming drink with the added health benefits of chaga to get you through the coldest winter days.

Place the chaga and spices in a medium pot with 8 cups water and simmer for 3 hours. The liquid should reduce by about half. Top up with more water halfway through, if needed. Strain and reserve the chaga chunk for a later use.

Heat the milk in a small pot with the sugar and tea bags. Steep for a few minutes. Remove the tea bags and whisk vigorously to create a frothy milk-tea blend.

Fill a mug halfway with the hot chaga liquid and top with the frothy chai milk tea.

PHOTO CREDITS

Café photos by Kara O'Keefe: pages 31, 70-1, 159.

Recipe photos by Geoff Pevlin: pages 9, 11, 12, 13, 18, 19, 21, 26-7, 28, 36, 38-9, 50, 55, 58, 61, 63, 67, 68, 73, 74, 81, 91, 96, 100, 103, 104, 106-7, 108, 111, 112, 119, 121, 131, 133, 134, 138-9, 140, 142, 144-5, 146, 149, 154.

Recipe photos by Nick Van Mele: pages 16, 17, 25, 32, 49, 77, 93, 94-5, 115, 117, 137, 151, 143, 157.

Ritche Perez: nettles, page 30.

All other photos taken by Murray extended family members.

Clockwise from lower left: Evan Murray, Nick Van Mele, Sylvia Bermudez, Brian Kowalski, Michael Murray, Susan Murray, Tim Murray, Nico Bermudez-Murray, Cameron Murray, Bobo, and Nanners.

INDEX

Sunflower
First Sunrise

Murray Meadows Farm
Portugal Cove, NL
Canada

Carrots
Long Tickle

Murray Meadows Farm
Portugal Cove, NL
Canada

Snap Peas
Cove King

Murray Meadows Farm
Portugal Cove, NL
Canada

Tomato
Avalon Beef

Murray Meadows Farm
Portugal Cove, NL
Canada